Critical Literacy Across the K–6 Curriculum

Through stories from kindergarten to sixth-grade classrooms where students and teachers have attempted to put a critical edge on their teaching, this book shows critical literacy in action across the curriculum. Readers see students and teachers together using critical literacy discourse to frame conversations in ways that engage students in examining the meaning of the texts they read and acting on local and global social issues that emerge.

Drawing on multiple perspectives, such as cross-curricular explorations, multimedia, and child-centered inquiry pedagogies, the text features a theoretical toolkit; demonstrations from across the content areas, including art, music, and media literacy; integration of technology; and attention to how critical literacy can inform decisions about standards and assessment. Annotated booklists, examples of students' work, "Reflection Questions," "Try This" (practical classroom strategies), and "Resource Boxes" can be used to encourage and support engaging in critical literacy work in different areas of the curriculum.

Vivian Maria Vasquez is Professor, School of Education, American University, USA.

Critical Literacy Across the K–6 Curriculum

VIVIAN MARIA VASQUEZ

Routledge
Taylor & Francis Group
NEW YORK AND LONDON

First published 2017
by Routledge
711 Third Avenue, New York, NY 10017

and by Routledge
2 Park Square, Milton Park, Abingdon, Oxon, OX14 4RN

Routledge is an imprint of the Taylor & Francis Group, an informa business

Library of Congress Cataloging-in-Publication Data
A catalog record for this book has been requested

ISBN: 978-1-138-18848-8 (hbk)
ISBN: 978-1-138-18849-5 (pbk)
ISBN: 978-1-315-64227-7 (ebk)

Typeset in Dutch823 BT
by Apex CoVantage, LLC

To Andy and TJ
Now and always.

Brief Contents

Contents

About the Author

Vivian Vasquez is a professor in the School of Education at American University, Washington, DC, USA, where she teaches courses in critical literacy, children's literature, and early childhood education. Prior to this she was a public school and preschool teacher for 14 years. She received her doctorate from Indiana University, Bloomington, USA; her masters from Mount Saint Vincent University in Halifax, Nova Scotia, Canada; and her undergraduate degrees from the University of Toronto, Ontario, Canada, and from Lakehead University, Thunder Bay, Ontario. At the release of this book, she will have worked as an educator for over 30 years.

Vivian has held appointive and elected positions at the International Reading Association, the National Council of Teachers of English, the Whole Language Umbrella, and the American Educational Research Association (AERA). Other honors include winning the James N. Britton Award for her book *Negotiating Critical Literacies With Young Children*. This book also received the AERA Division B Outstanding Book Award.

Vivian was born in the Philippines, grew up in Canada, and currently lives in Maryland, USA, with her pride and joy, her son, Taylor, and her husband, Andy.

Author Information for Correspondence

You can reach Vivian at vvasque@american.edu. You can also visit her website at www.vivianvasquez.com and view her podcast on critical literacy at www.clippodcast.com.

About the Cover Art

I am most grateful for the beautiful cover art for this book, which was created by Jerome C. Harste. He describes the art piece in this way.

> This goat is made out of bar codes. My thoughts during the creation of this piece of art is that our society so inscribes us with print that it is hard to tell ourselves from our environment, especially as we get dazzled by the colors and motifs that bombard us. The message I wanted to convey is that to be 21st century literate we need to become critically aware of how we have been and are being inscribed. I purposefully made the goat young, suggesting that it is never too early to begin the process of becoming more critically literate.
>
> J.C.H.

Aside from his wonderful description, I also love Jerry's subtle layering of several images, including letters, musical notes, and numbers alongside the bar codes and the dazzling colors—a wonderful representation of critical literacy across the curriculum. Thank you so much, Jerry!

Acknowledgments

I would like to thank my colleagues who contributed to this book through sharing with me stories of work they have done in their settings: Susan Adamson, David Chiola-Nakai, Carol Felderman, Lee Heffernan, Kevan Miller, Michael Muise, Janice Shear, Bryan Woods, and Sarah Vander Zanden. Their insight and willingness to negotiate spaces for critical literacies in various contexts using different texts are an inspiration to us all. My deepest gratitude also goes to the children whose learning is described in this book, including Daniella, Jacob, Maisie, and Elle for sharing their song lyrics. Thanks to Vera J. Lee for reviewing the proposal for this book. Thank you to my Facebook friends and colleagues who graciously responded to my crowdsourcing requests while I was in the midst of writing. There are too many of you to list here, but your ongoing support is greatly appreciated.

This book was written with invaluable colleagues and friends in mind. There are now so many of you, but some have been with me for a long time—specifically, Jerry Harste, Andy Manning, Barbara Comber, Allan Luke, Hilary Janks, Sonia Nieto, and Naomi Silverman. It has been such an honor to keep your company all these years. Naomi, you always recognize the potential in work that I do. Thank you for your ongoing encouragement and support. Thank you also to the Routledge team for your work on my books through the years.

A special thank you to my family in Canada and the USA—for always being there for me. Andy, thank you for your "go for it" attitude, ongoing support, and technical help. TJ, you make it all worthwhile—now and always.

About This Book

In this book you will find stories of my own experience in the classroom as well as the stories shared with me by classroom teachers who are colleagues and friends as we each embarked on a journey of exploring what critical literacy could afford our teaching and our students' learning. Like me, these teachers also wanted to know what difference it would make to frame our teaching from this perspective. They wanted to know what kinds of literate learners could be produced from this practice.

Consequently, this book is a collection of stories from kindergarten through sixth-grade classrooms where students and teachers have attempted to put a critical edge on their teaching. It consists of detailed critical literacy events and instances from classrooms as well as practical classroom strategies (labeled "Try This" throughout the book) and resources (labeled "Resource Boxes" within the chapters) that can be used as sources to encourage and support engaging in critical literacy work in different areas of the curriculum.

Over the years there have been a growing number of accounts of critical literacy work in classrooms (Comber, 2001b; Morgan, 1997; O'Brien, 2001; Vasquez, 1994, 1998, 2001b, 2005a). Very limited in the literature, however, are accounts of critical literacies across the curriculum in K–6 settings that include the use of media literacy and technology. I hope this book contributes to filling that gap. In particular I hope reading this book and engaging in some of the ideas presented become opportunities for you to explore possibilities for critical literacy in different content areas across the curriculum.

How This Book Was Conceptualized

There are numerous publications that speak to teaching and learning across the curriculum in K–6 settings. Most speak in general terms and are not necessarily framed from a particular orientation or perspective. When I decided to write this book with a focus on critical literacies across the curriculum, a priority became how to do this and stay true to my belief in creating critical curricula using topics and issues that emerge through living, learning, and teaching in K–6 settings. As such what you will find is that, although each chapter places at center a particular content or subject area, in each of the stories shared, coming to that content or subject area is a result of drawing from the children's interests and creating learning opportunities that build from those interests rather than building from a content area such as mathematics or social studies. The content areas therefore are used to give perspective to the work at hand. As such, children engage in learning through different lenses, such as those of mathematicians, scientists, and musicians. Further, although each chapter centers on a particular area, it is important to note the ways in which various subject areas intersect. I have included Resource Box A.1 to demonstrate this. Working across the curriculum in this way creates a much smoother and often seamless flow between the subject areas. It is also not the case that while doing cross-curricular work one must 'cover' every content area. If we did this, we would likely be spending more time planning than teaching and learning.

Resource Box A.1 Intersections Across the Content Areas

Content Areas	Topics Under Study and Intersections in Different Areas of the Curriculum			
	White Wash **Chapter 2**	**Mountie Poster Chapter 3**	**Weather Song Chapter 5**	**Hoops Issue Chapter 12**
Science			Learning about weather	Gender Differences
Social Studies	Racism over time	History of the RCMP		Gender Stereotypes
Math		Making sure there is an equitable representation of males and females	Creating a new weather graph and survey	
Language Arts	Picture book study and writer's workshop	Reading books about the RCMP	Reading books and writing the weather song	Researching and writing scripts and letters
Art Drama Music	Choosing book illustrations to represent thinking	Re-designing the Mountie Musical Ride poster and acting out riding on a horse	Revising the weather song	Performing public service announcements
Physical Education and Health			Discussion of weather and dressing for different weather	Hoops issue that arose during physical education class
Technology	Depictions of race in movies		Creating a video about the new weather graph	Creating public service announcements

Figures and Tables

Figures

Tables

1

Teaching and Learning From a Critical Literacy Perspective

Patricia:	Are you sure you looked?
Alexandro:	Everywhere in there!
Patricia:	She [the librarian] even helped me. She said, "I guess we don't have any."
Alexandro:	Did you tell her that's not fair?

It was November. My kindergarten students and I had been together for three months and had gotten to know one another quite well. During this time I had attempted to construct a critical literacy curriculum and make use of pedagogy to create opportunities for inquiry learning, culturally relevant teaching, and for us to engage in a dialogue about diversity using the varied linguistic and cultural experiences and resources that this ethnically diverse group of children brought to the classroom. The brief conversation between Patricia and Alexandro (the names of students that appear in this volume are pseudonyms) took place one day after returning from a visit to our school library. They had been looking for a book on the Philippines as one way to support Emma, a new student in the class, whose family had just moved to Canada from the Philippines. Their quest was met with frustration when they learned there were no books with characters that might be Filipino, nor were there any resource books on the Philippines. In a sense these children were learning about the notion of being "other," of not having spaces, places, and opportunities to belong. Patricia and Alexandro's frustration led me to suggest a class project focusing on the question: Do we see ourselves in books that are in our school library? I did this believing that engaging in such collaborative, collective meaning-making work could contribute to re-shaping what Comber (2016) refers to as their local place, making it a more accessible and welcoming place for students such as Emma.

A topic such as this may seem too difficult or complex for young children. However, from the beginning of the school year my students had available to them more powerful ways of talking about the world as I framed my teaching from a critical literacy perspective. As such they immediately read against the hegemonic library practice of ordering books without really knowing who potential readers would be.

A long-held intention of mine has been to find ways of creating spaces for my students to participate in the world differently. So at the end of the school year, I ask myself: Are my students able to participate in the world differently as a result of the work we have done throughout the year? If the answer is no, then I need to ask myself: What have I taught them and what of those things is of any importance to their lives? A critical literacy perspective is one theoretical tool that affords pedagogical practices that create spaces for my students to engage in ways that allow them to participate differently in the world. The fact that I build curriculum from their interests means that it becomes more likely that the work we do will have importance in their lives.

Luke (2014) describes critical literacy as "the object of a half-century of theoretical debate and practical innovation in the field of education" (p. 21). Part of the debate is a response to attempts by some educators and researchers to pin down a specific definition for it. There is a belief among many critical literacy theorists and educators (Comber & Simpson, 2001; Comber & Thomson, 2001; Luke, 2007; Vasquez, 2001a, 2004) that as a framework for engaging in literacy work, it should look, feel, and sound different, and it should accomplish different sorts of life work depending on the context and place in which it is being used as a perspective for teaching and learning. In other publications, I have referred to this framing as a way of being, where I have argued that critical literacy should not be an add-on but a frame through which to participate in the world (Vasquez, 1994, 2000a, 2000b, 2000c, 2010, 2014a). As such, there is no such thing as a critical literacy text. Rather, there are texts through which we may better be able to create spaces for critical literacies. Such texts are shared and discussed throughout this book.

The world as text, however, can be read from a critical literacy perspective. What this means is that issues and topics of interest that capture students' interests as they participate in the world around them can and should be used as text to build a curriculum that has significance in their lives. In spite of the fact that critical literacy does not have a set definition or a normative history, the following key aspects have been described in the literature. It should be noted that such key aspects or tenets would likely take different shape depending on one's orientation to critical literacy.

- Critical literacy should be looked on as a lens, frame, or perspective for teaching throughout the day rather than as a topic to be covered or a unit to be studied. What this means is that critical literacy involves having a critical perspective or way of being. As of this writing, demonstrations of critical literacy in the English/ Language Arts curriculum dominate. However, there is a slowly growing number of accounts across the curriculum and in the content areas, such as science, social studies, and mathematics.
- Students learn best when what they are learning has importance in their lives. As such, using the topics, issues, and questions that they raise should be an important part of creating the classroom curriculum. Further, while working across the curriculum in the content areas, diverse students' cultural knowledge (drawn from inside the classroom and the children's everyday worlds, homes, and communities) and multimodal literacy practices should be used to build curriculum (Comber, 2001c, 2016; Vasquez, 1998, 2000c, 2010, 2017).
- From a critical literacy perspective, the world is seen as a socially constructed text that can be read. As such no text is ever neutral. What this means is that all texts are created from a particular perspective with the intention of conveying particular messages. Such texts work to position readers in certain ways. We therefore need to question the perspectives

of others. The earlier students are introduced to this idea, the sooner they are able to understand what it means to be researchers of language and explore ways texts can be revised, rewritten, or reconstructed to shift or reframe the message(s) conveyed.

- Texts work to have us think about and believe certain things in specific ways. However, just as texts are never neutral, the ways we read text are also never neutral. Each time we read, write or create, we draw from our past experiences and understanding about how the world works. We therefore should also analyze our own readings of texts and unpack the position(s) from which we engage in reading such texts.
- Discourses—ways of being, doing, and acting—mediate our lives. This means we live our lives based on our understanding of the world and the perspectives, ideologies, and beliefs that shape that understanding. How we make meaning in the world happens through these ways of being, doing, and acting.
- Critical literacy work should focus on social issues, such as race, class, or gender, and the ways in which we use language and images to shape our understanding of these issues. As such part of this work should involve making sense of the sociopolitical systems through which such issues play out and through which we live our lives and also questioning these systems.
- Critical literacy practices can be transformative and contribute to change inequitable ways of being, problematic social practices, and the places and spaces in which we live our lives.
- Students who engage in critical literacy from a young age are likely going to be better able to contribute to a more equitably and socially just world by being better able to make informed decisions regarding such issues as power and control.
- Text design and production, the creation or construction of multimodal texts, and the decisions that are part of that process are essential to critical literacy work and can provide opportunities for transformation. This includes the notion that it is not sufficient to simply create texts for the sake of "practicing a skill." If students are to create texts, they ought to be able to let those texts do the work intended. For instance, if students are writing surveys or creating petitions, they should be done with real-life intent for the purpose of

dealing with a real issue. If students write petitions, they should be able to send them to whomever they were intended.

- Finally, critical literacy is about imagining thoughtful ways of thinking about reconstructing and redesigning texts and images to convey different and more socially just and equitable messages that have real-life effects. This work should make use of multimodal literacies and students' multilingual capacities to make meaning in the world using combinations of print-based text and music, art, or technologically based text, such as websites, videos, or podcasts.

Do We See Ourselves in Books That Are in Our School Library?

The project that grew out of the conversation at the beginning of this chapter was an important one that raised questions of moral responsibility and established the role that our class could play in negotiating new, more equitable social spaces in our school and beyond.

Our school was pre-K to eighth grade, with approximately 800 students. It was located in a middle-income neighborhood in a suburb of Toronto, Ontario, Canada. In our class of 18 students, we had 11 ethnicities represented, including children from Malta, the Philippines, and Peru. Many of the children spoke more than one language. The children and I were therefore disturbed when we searched through the shelves of our school library over the next few weeks and discovered the following:

- There were no books on the Philippines.
- The books on Peru were outdated and were published in the 1970s.
- There were no books on Malta.

Earlier in the school year, I talked to the children about acting on issues that were of concern to us—that is, doing something about problems we face in the spaces we inhabit, in the school community and beyond, to contribute to building more democratic ways of being and doing and more democratic spaces and places in which to live and do such things. At that time we made a list of possible types of actions, including finding out as much as we could about an issue to discuss and analyze it in a critical way.

We talked about writing letters, doing research to find more information on a topic, and asking to meet with individuals involved to make our concerns public. We also looked at our own ways of doing and saying things and how we may have contributed to existing problems by not acting on them.

To address our concern regarding the lack of culturally diverse books in our school library, we engaged in a conversation regarding possible solutions. One suggestion made by a group of students was to write a letter to the librarian (see Figure 1.1). The letter makes public the findings of the students' discoveries in the library. Along with the letter, we attached a list of books with characters from diverse ethnicities and backgrounds and multilingual books that could be purchased for our school library. This list was created by one of the boys in the class together with his parents. The children imagined that having such books in the library would make it a more accessible and welcoming place for diverse learners. They saw this project as ongoing—meaning that we would need to re-visit the books available in the library as the student population became increasingly diverse.

Dear____________
Our class did
research
in the library
on books.
This is what
we found out.
The other paper
has books you
should buy.

FIG. 1.1 Letter to the Librarian

The librarian was very receptive to the letter. When presented with the findings, she appeared genuinely disturbed that she had not realized the gaps in the book collections at our school library. Our work helped her to re-think her practice of ordering books to ensure that books she ordered were diverse and would serve the needs of the culturally and linguistically diverse children in our school. Like many people, she had not thought about the marginalization of certain individuals and groups and the inaccessibility of the library for students who are unable to see themselves in books and other texts used in school. She immediately worked on ordering books to address our concerns. She also began rethinking the decisions she made regarding which books to display based on who is represented and not represented by those books.

As part of our project, we created a newsletter outlining the work that we had done. This newsletter was taken home by students and was one way of filtering our class inquiry into some of the children's homes. From the newsletter, Mena and her family began to explore how different cultures are represented by the way in which books are displayed at local bookstores. She and her parents talked to the manager of their neighborhood bookstore, emphasizing the need for books that represent diverse cultures to be available all year, not just for special events such as Black History Month or Women's History Month. Anthony and his mother questioned why children's literature was hidden in the back corner of their local bookstore and why a computer used to locate books was not available in the children's section as it was in other areas. It was amazing to learn about ways that my students had taken what they had learned in the classroom into their homes to engage in projects with their parents. In a way they had become researchers of their world. Researching their world involved asking questions, finding out answers, sharing those answers, and then disseminating or sharing their ideas in ways that influence and shape their local spaces (Comber, 2016). In our case they contributed to transforming our school library into a more welcoming space for children from diverse cultural backgrounds.

Currently as a professor at the School of Education at American University I continue to work with classroom teachers and preschool and elementary school children. Prior to this, I was a preschool and elementary school teacher for 14 years, and as such I explored ways of framing curriculum from a critical literacy perspective. Common to both experiences are the connections I have kept with other classroom teachers. The motivation to connect was an interest in creating spaces for critical literacy.

Using Critical Literacies to Get Things Done in the World

In the opening vignette, we enter the kindergarten classroom where Patricia and Alexandro led the charge for changing the kinds of books that were made available in our school library. As they engaged in this act, they helped to break the pattern of privileging some students (those students who find themselves in books) while marginalizing others (those students, like Emma, whose experiences are not represented in the books available in the school library). In so doing our school's book collection became much more culturally relevant for the children and their families.

The work we did is reflective of Comber's (1992) findings that in classrooms where a critical literacy position is advocated, teachers respect student resistance, explore minority culture constructions of literacy and language, and problematize classroom and public text. To respect student resistance and explore minority culture constructions of literacy and language, teachers provide space in the curriculum to address the diverse needs of students, including ensuring the curriculum speaks to the cultural ways of being of the students and the varied discourses (experiences with literacy, literate ways of being, and language use) that those students bring to the classroom and that this happens across the curriculum. In our library project, for instance, we researched the lack of representation of particular groups of people in the books available at our school library. While problematizing classroom and public texts, teachers help students to interrupt and analyze texts that are often considered natural or neutral. For example, students and teachers together look closely at the illustrations and choice of words used in texts such as books and magazine advertisements. In our library project we disrupted the common practice of having on offer only those books representing the most dominant groups of people in our school as part of our school library book collections. The library project is an example of what happens when classroom work is framed from a socially critical approach to teaching and learning. Through this approach or perspective, students become or are positioned as researchers of language. In other publications I forefront the negotiation of critical literacies using everyday issues raised by my students (Vasquez, 2003a, 2003b, 2004, 2005a, 2005b), work that integrates the use of children's books (Vasquez, 2010), or work that makes use of technology (Vasquez & Felderman, 2013).

Working From a Theory of Language and Learning

The opening vignette offers a number of important insights into teaching and learning from a critical literacy perspective. When I asked Patricia and Alexandro why they felt it was important to have books on the Philippines or books that included characters who look Filipino, they offered two reasons. First, they said that having books on the Philippines was one way for them to learn about a country, and second, if there were no books with Filipino-looking characters, then it might be harder for Emma to tell her stories. When asked to clarify what "telling her stories" meant, they explained, "That means that Emma can say 'like in my home' or 'like when this happened to me or that happened to me' or 'that's not what I think,' and if there's no books with Philippines people then it'll be hard to say that." They continued by suggesting, "It isn't fair that other people are in books and Emma isn't." In other words, Patricia and Alexandro recognized that books present different kinds of realities, providing spaces for readers to connect their own experiences and understanding for purposes of reaffirming those experiences and understandings, or for taking issue with the realities that are presented for them. Further, they recognize that particular students' experiences and understandings are marginalized when they do not find themselves in books or when the realities presented do not represent their experiences.

Patricia and Alexandro are developing a critical perspective in the way that they use language to critique and in the way that they critique the language and images in books. How did they come to this perspective? In a sense, they have come to learn how to use language to critique in great part because of the critical discourses or analytical ways of being that have been made available to them in the classroom. For me, these ways of being are shaped in large part by the theoretical toolkit that informs my teaching and subsequently some of the discourses (ways of being, doing, and talking) that my students learn.

Building a Theoretical Toolkit

I cut my critical literacy teeth in 1993 while taking a graduate course through Mount Saint Vincent University, which was being held during the summer at the University of South Australia. While in Australia my classmates and I had an opportunity to work with Barbara Comber and spend time with Jenny O'Brien. Barbara was finishing her doctorate with Allan Luke and exploring notions of critical literacy with him. She was also working with Jenny on creating opportunities for critical literacies in her classroom. At the time I had been framing my teaching from an inquiry-based perspective driven by whole-language principles (Watson, Burke, & Harste, 1989).

The more I talked with Barbara and thought about the kind of work Jenny was doing in her classroom, such as using Mother's Day ads as text, the more I imagined possibilities for critical literacy in my own classroom. Using their work in critical literacy as a lens through which to revisit some of my teaching practices led me to the realization that I was, on many instances, engaging in a naïve form of literacy teaching whereby I marginalized the social issues that my students were raising (Vasquez, 1994). In some instances, I downright ignored them. After that summer I was determined to listen to and observe differently what my students said and did and to attend more closely to the artifacts of their world that were interesting to them with an eye for opportunities to create spaces for critical literacy. For instance, while teaching kindergartners, one of my students questioned the use of toy packaging included in a fast food chain's kid's meal. Using the kid's meal as an artifact of learning, we deconstructed and analyzed the information on the packaging, asking questions like, "Who would want this information? Why? What are the words and images on the package attempting to do to me as a consumer?" (For more on this topic, refer to Vasquez, 2005b.) Barbara's work on negotiating critical literacies became part of my theoretical toolkit as I began to imagine possibilities for doing with my students social justice work in literacy. This imagining led me to read the work of Freire and other critical pedagogues (Edelsky, 2000; Freire, 1972; Freire & Macedo, 1987; Shor & Freire, 1987). Freire pushed me to think of what it means to "read the world" (Freire & Macedo, 1987, p. 29) and not just the word. He led me to be concerned about raising the "conscientizacao [critical consciousness] of learners" (Larson & Marsh, 2005, p. 41). However, Freire's work was primarily focused on adult learners and did not deal specifically with classroom practice, so I was thrilled when Luke and Freebody

(1999a) began their work on what came to be known as the Four Resources Model (refer to www.readingonline.org/research/luke-freebody.html for more information about the model).

In their model, Luke and Freebody (1999b) assert that literacy is never neutral—that literacy is always situated within a series of ideologies or beliefs that shape what we do. While developing their model, they examined existing and proposed literacy curricula and pedagogical strategies. They state that effective literacy draws from a repertoire of practices that allow learners, as they engage in reading and writing activities, to participate in various "families of literate practices" (Luke & Freebody, 1999a, p. 6). Freebody and Luke use the term *practices* to denote work that is actually done by literate beings in classrooms and beyond as an indication that these are negotiated, carried out, and achieved in everyday contexts, unlike terms such as *schemata* or *competencies*, which denote a more individual, psychological model of literacy. In the Four Resources Model, four dynamic and fluid "families of (social) practices" (p. 6) are described.

1. Code-breaking practices. These practices refer to having access to the skills required to break the code of written texts by recognizing and using fundamental features and architecture, including alphabet, sounds in words, spelling, and structural conventions and patterns.
2. Practices that provide opportunities to participate with text. These practices involve participating in understanding and composing meaningful written, visual, and spoken texts, taking into account each text's interior meaning systems in relation to a reader's available knowledge and experiences of other cultural discourses, texts, and meaning systems.
3. Practices for using text. These practices involve using texts functionally by knowing about and acting on the different cultural and social functions that various texts perform inside and outside school and understanding that these functions shape the way texts are structured, their tone, their degree of formality, and their sequence of components.
4. Practices that create space for the critical analysis of text. These practices involve the critical analysis and transformation of texts by acting on knowledge that texts are not ideologically natural or neutral—that they represent particular points of views while silencing others, and they influence people's ideas—and that their designs and discourses can be critiqued and redesigned in novel and hybrid ways.

Each family of practices is needed for literacy learning, but none in isolation is sufficient. Each of the four is inclusive, with each being integral to the achievement of the others.

In the 1970s and 1980s, psycholinguistic and schema theory emphasized reader–text interactions, drawing attention to text–meaning practices or, more specifically, the construction of a reader who used textual and personal resources to coproduce a meaningful reading. In the late 1980s and early 1990s, sociolinguistic and sociosemiotic theory focused attention on language in use during which reading was viewed in terms of what it did or could accomplish pragmatically in the real world. Luke and Freebody (1999b) assert that reading should be seen as a non-neutral form of cultural practice, one that positions readers in advantageous and disadvantageous ways. They argue that readers need to be able to interrogate the assumptions and ideologies that are embedded in text as well as the assumptions that they, as sociocultural beings, bring to the text. This leads to asking questions such as, "Whose voice is heard? Who is silenced? Whose reality is presented? Whose reality is ignored? Who is advantaged? Who is disadvantaged?" These sorts of questions open spaces for analyzing the discourses or ways of being that maintain certain social practices over others. The Four Resources Model was an important tool for analyzing what sort of literacy practices I was privileging and marginalizing in the classroom. It was clear that teaching from a critical literacy perspective would produce a very different learner who could make more informed decisions in the world. A useful framework for me to think about what kinds of literate beings I want my students to become in the world is Harste's (2001) Halliday Plus Model of language learning. (See Resource Box 1.1 at the end of the chapter.)

The Halliday Plus Model builds on what we already know about language, making use of what has worked and problematizing what hasn't worked. It is based on a belief that literacy is socially constructed and that when different ways of being are made available, literacy can be reconstructed. It begs the questions, "What discourses maintain certain social practices? For what purpose? To whose advantage?" It also builds on the notion of individuals being multiliterate and that there is not just one literacy but different literacies that allow different access in a variety of contexts and spaces in the world. In a practical sense, this means that it is not enough for children to learn language, to learn about language, and to learn through language, but that children also need to learn to use language to critique (Harste, 2001). According to Egawa and Harste (2001),

> The ability to sound out words and make meaning from texts makes children good consumers rather than good citizens. To be truly literate, children need to understand how texts work and that they as literate beings have options in terms of how they are going to respond to a particular text in a given setting.
>
> (p. 2)

In conversations with other educators regarding the work they do in helping children to understand how texts work, a common denominator has been the use of critical analysis, often referred to as deconstructing text or unpacking text. Less common is what is done *after* the critique, deconstructing, or unpacking. Critical analysis without action seems to keep us in the same place as when we started. In other words, it is the action piece, doing something with what we discover through critical analysis of text that helps us to participate differently in the world. Hilary Janks was instrumental in helping me to articulate this thinking. She has written about an interdependent model of critical literacy that includes text design or redesign as an essential component of critical literacy work. She notes that central to this work is helping children to understand the relationship between language and power (Janks, 2000)—namely, that particular discursive practices (ways of talking, doing, being, and acting) carry more or less power or influence in different settings and places. Janks explains that different realizations of critical literacy operate with different conceptions of this relation by foregrounding one orientation or other of domination, access, diversity, or design. Focusing only on one orientation is problematic. For instance, if a curriculum claims to be framed from a difference and diversity perspective but does not simultaneously address issues of dominance, then particular perspectives tend to be privileged while others are marginalized. If this curriculum is not also oriented toward issues of access, then how do we make accessible to our students and help them understand dominant forms that will help them participate differently and more powerfully in the world? Janks argues that these orientations are interdependent. Figure 1.2 is a representation of my understanding of Janks' model. I use arrows among the circles of domination, access, diversity, and design to show the interconnections among these orientations. At the center is a reminder of the larger sociocultural framework of reading the world as text through which each of the orientations intersects and connect. Circling the

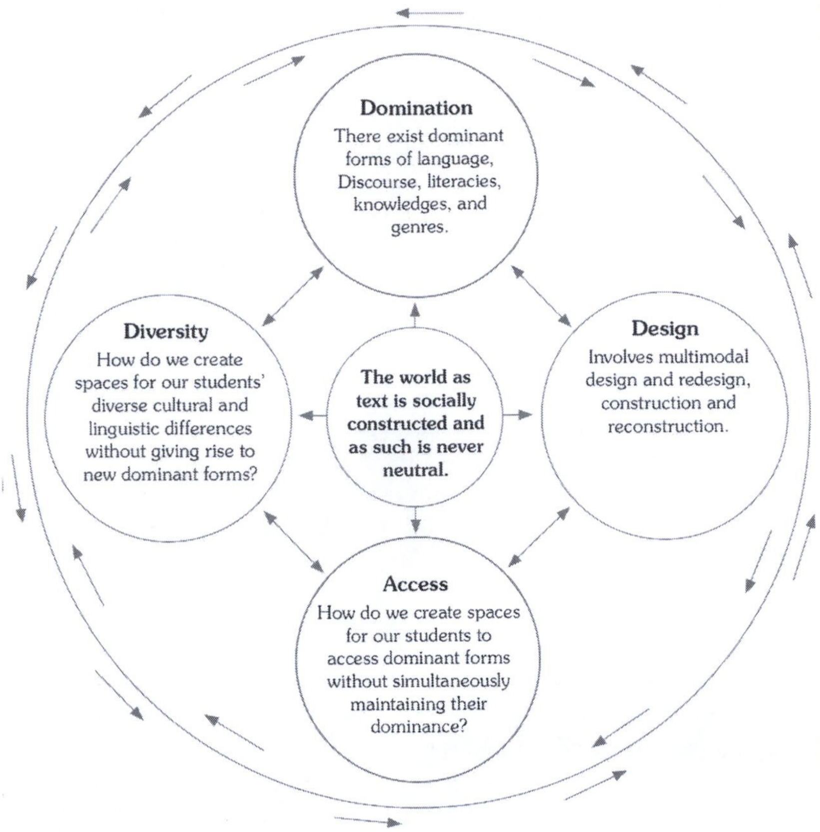

FIG. 1.2 Janks' Model

orientations are arrows that point clockwise and counterclockwise, denoting that there is no sequence or order through which to take up these orientations. Rather, we move fluidly through and between each.

In my teaching, I have for years attempted to create or negotiate class projects with my students that have real-world effects. My book *Negotiating Critical Literacies With Young Children* (Vasquez, 2014b) contains several examples of what these projects are like in classrooms with very young learners. However, I am always on the lookout for new ways for students to represent their projects, their thinking, their understandings, and their ideas. This is where the new literacies and new technologies take a place in my theoretical toolkit. Work done in new literacies and new technologies by people like Buckingham and Sefton-Green (1995), Gee (2003), Lankshear and Knobel (2007), and Marsh (2005) have helped me to think through notions of design and redesign and the role these play in creating opportunities to participate in the world differently. Most recently Comber (2016) has impacted my thinking through her articulation of place-based pedagogies as cross-curricular practices that could create powerful spaces for children to engage in complex meaning making that allows them to connect with their places, their environments, and each other.

In the next chapter, we enter a third-grade space and meet Lee Heffernan, who shares her experience in using a six-step strategy that she developed for taking up social issues such as racism using what Harste (2003) refers to as "social issues texts" (p. 9). In chapter three I focus on transformative writing with a group of kindergarten students that I worked with and a group of fifth-grade students taught by Janice Shear. These children participated as analysts of their world who used writing as a tool for making visible or disrupting problematic practices in their settings. In chapter 4 I focus on critical literacy and math as we spend time with Michael Muise and his fifth- and sixth-grade students. Together they worked to understand and disrupt what they saw as unfair school practices, using math as a way to advance their agenda of planning an alternative end-of-the-year celebration.

The next group we meet is Kevan Miller and her first-grade students. In this fifth chapter I explore ways that Kevan negotiated critical literacies using science observations. In particular, we become privy to the work her students did to interrogate, deconstruct, re-write, and perform a long-standing but problematic 'weather song' that is part of the first-grade curriculum. In chapter 6 we spend time with Sarah Vander Zanden and her fifth-grade students and their critical literacy work in the social studies curriculum. In the chapter we learn about the work the children did to disrupt problematic Arbor Day routines at their school, which led them to realize the importance of taking social action to resist, disrupt, and reimagine problematic social practices and school policies. In the next chapter we meet a group of third graders and their teacher Susan Adamson, who attempted to create opportunities for her students to make sense of their world through deconstructing and analyzing picture books. This seventh chapter focuses on using drama to engage critically with the book *White Wash*. Process drama became a vehicle for them to embody the issues of racism with which they were grappling.

Chapter 8 focuses on getting critical with music. In this chapter I share instances of children between 3 and 9 years of age using music in varied ways to negotiate meaning in the world. I also share the story of a group of children in Kent, England, who engaged in social action by using music as a way to save their school from being closed down due to lack of funds. In chapter 9 I focus on engaging in powerful and pleasurable critical literacies with a group of 4- to 7-year-old children by using art and everyday popular culture texts. In the chapter I share how the children engaged in exploring the world of buyers, sellers, and the consumer world through art and re-design. In chapter 10 I focus on critical media literacy while spending time with David Chiola-Nakai's sixth-grade students and Bryan Woods pre-kindergarten and kindergarten students. The sixth graders work on deconstructing and analyzing Nike texts while the younger children work on unpacking Father's Day ads. Both groups engage in this work as a way to grow in their understanding of the powerful influence of media in our world. In the next chapter I take you into Carol Felderman's second-grade classroom, where together we created, produced, and made accessible to a worldwide audience a podcast (online broadcast). In this eleventh chapter I share both the process of podcasting as well as the transformative effects of having participated in such an endeavor.

Chapter 12 takes us into new spaces for exploring critical literacies—the physical education and health education curricula. First we visit with Christine Paul's third-grade students and their work at disrupting gender stereotypes during physical education class. Following this we spend time with a group of preschoolers with whom I worked to explore the discourses and image selections used in food packaging with an eye for re-designing the packaging. Finally, in chapter 13 I pull the chapters together and share thoughts regarding the book as a whole.

At the end of each chapter I have included "Reflection Questions" as well as "Try This" ideas for you to try out in your setting. These are ways that I hope will create spaces for you to connect the ideas in this book with your experiences, and as one way to help you imagine ways of creating spaces for critical literacies across the curriculum.

I hope that the versions of classroom life presented in the following chapters can complement or encourage the vision you have for engaging in powerful ways with critical literacies across the curriculum, to contribute to creating a more equitably just and fair world for us all.

Reflection Questions

1. Obtain a journal in which to write any thoughts, comments, connections, or questions as you read this book. Begin by reflecting on your own experience as a young learner. What kinds of texts do you recall reading while you were an elementary school student? In what ways did the texts that were made available to you reflect your own experiences? In what ways were the texts that were made available to you inconsistent with your own experiences? What were some of the ways that you talked about these texts? What purpose did they serve in your life? Were any of them multimodal (films, songs, everyday text . . .) or were they primarily books? Were these texts that could be used in different areas of the curriculum?
2. Make a list of all the children in your classroom, noting their cultural backgrounds. Then walk around the classroom paying close attention to the children's available resources (books and other materials). Write about how closely the resources in your classroom reflect the cultural makeup of your students. For instance, what can you say about the consistencies or inconsistencies between your students' backgrounds and experiences and the backgrounds and experiences of the characters in the books you make available to those students?
3. Together with your students, make a list of books that you feel should be added to your classroom or school library to ensure that all the children in the class are reflected in the books available to them. It would be very useful to add to this list throughout the school year.
4. How are you using language in your classroom? Situate your own literacy teaching by noting in what ways you are using language in your classroom using the following four categories: (1) things that I do to teach language, (2) things that I do to teach about language, (3) things that I do to help my students learn through language, and (4) things that I do to help my students use language critically.
5. In your journal, reflect on your current theory of language and learning. Begin by naming your theory of language and learning and then write about how what you do in the classroom reflects or is inconsistent with what say you believe. This naming is an important step in rethinking and changing

our practice because often our ideologies or beliefs become so much a part of who we are that they become invisible to us. Naming helps to make our theories visible, therefore making these easier for us to reflect and act on more critically.

Try This

- Have a look at the Halliday Plus Model (Resource Box 1.1) at the end of this chapter.
- Take a sheet of paper and fold it so that you have four sections in which to jot down notes.
- Use these four headings, one in each quadrant: Learning Language, Learning About Language, Learning Through Language, and Learning to Use Language to Critique.
- In each quadrant jot down your teaching practices that reflect each particular element of the Halliday Plus Model.
- What did you find? Which boxes are most filled? Which are the least filled?
- What are some things you might try in your setting in order to engage your students in using language to critique and re-design?

Resource Box 1.1 Halliday Plus Model

Adapted from Harste, (2001). The Halliday Plus Model. *School Talk* 7(1), p. 2.

Learning Language

Using language and other sign systems as a meaning-making process.

Examples of using language to learn:

- Read-aloud
- Shared reading
- Partner reading
- Reader's theater
- Independent reading and writing
- Writer's notebook
- Big books
- Journals and reading logs

Learning About Language

Understanding how texts operate and how they are coded.

Examples of teaching practices that help students learn about language:

- Teaching letter-sound relationships
- Comprehension strategies
- Minilessons
- Demonstrations
- Focused lessons
- Class charts

Learning Through Language

Using reading and writing as tools and toys for learning about the world.

Examples of teaching practices that help children learn through language:

- Using text sets
- Reflective journals
- Literature study
- Inquiry or focused study
- Sketch to stretch
- Process drama

Learning to Use Language to Critique

Using language to question what seems normal and natural as well as to redesign and create alternate social worlds.

Examples of practices that create spaces for using language to critique and re-design:

- Social action projects
- Building off everyday texts and social issues
- Using texts that provide opportunities for interrogating the word and the world

2

Reading Critically

Louis:	In lots of movies, most of the main characters are white.
Kristen:	When you look in a book . . . no black people.
John:	Yeah.
Kristen:	When you look in a book, it's like, they're white, they're white, there and there and there . . . and like off in the distance, you find one African American girl.

Bringing the Outside World Into the Classroom

One morning, late in the month of May, the children in Lee Heffernan's third-grade public school classroom in a midwestern US town gathered at the rug to discuss *White Wash* (Shange, 1997). The story centers on a young African American girl, Helene-Angel, who is traumatized when a gang attacks her and her brother, Mauricio, on their way home from school. During the attack the gang members spray paint the little girl's face white, telling her they are doing her a good deed teaching her how to be White, teaching her how to be American.

In this opening exchange, Louis, Kristen, and John use an observation made by Louis regarding a majority of characters being white in movies he has watched, as a lens through which to talk about books. The exchange is an example of conversations that took place as Lee and her students shared their comments about things they notice in their experiences while at school, in their community, and in other places they visit. Subsequently this kind of exchange also resulted from questions and connections about such issues as the children raised them during class discussions. Lee notes that these somewhat challenging and sometimes uncomfortable discussions with her students were not like those she has had with them in the past. It seems that introducing particular kinds of children's books into the curriculum made the difference.

Critical Literacy and Children's Literature

Commonalities between books referred to as social issues books in the literature (Harste, Leland, Lewison, Ociepka, & Vasquez, 2000; Lewison, Leland, & Harste, 2014) create spaces for exploring social problems or conflicts, and provide opportunities to unpack issues that problematically position individuals or groups or issues that are opposed by individuals or groups within a society. *White Wash* (Shange, 1997), an example of this type of book, was one of several social issues books Lee shared with her students that she claimed shifted the ways in which she and her students were able to talk about books and more specifically the social issues embedded in those books.

As Lee read *White Wash*, she remembers her students eagerly anticipating an opportunity for response. From their previous experience studying picture books with Lee, they knew that the book would be the focus of their reading and writing for several days. They knew this was their teacher's way of bringing issues from their world outside of school into the classroom. Pedagogically, Lee created mini-lessons to teach specific concepts about a topic, to unpack or analyze texts such as books, or to teach specific skills.

When she first began reading books that focused on social issues, Lee was surprised by the complex conversations that resulted. She was initially hesitant to share such books, feeling that they may contain topics that might be too uncomfortable to discuss. In the end she felt the benefits would outweigh the potential discomfort. When she did begin reading social issues books to the children, they responded with such enthusiasm that she came to see books as important tools for bringing a critical perspective to their reading and writing workshop. The connections her students were making by focusing on social issues they were bringing into the classroom and connecting these to the literacy curriculum helped them to become more informed readers and writers. Lee recalls her initial experiences with such books.

> Lee: I began by spending several days talking about the books and came to see that lingering with a book over several days had some benefits. First, we were able to talk about a wide range of issues, rather than focusing on one or two main ideas or themes. Second, kids who tended to be quieter found their voice after several days and shared insights that we would have missed. Third, I was able to give myself more time to consider and develop issues from the book that seemed especially significant to all of us.

Lingering With a Book: Six Sessions With a Social Issues Text

Like Lisa Stanzi's second-grade students, whom she describes in her book about creating a literature-based reading curriculum (Galda, Rayburn, & Stanzi, 2000), Lee's students knew how they felt about certain books, they could comment and ask questions about those books, but they found engaging in sustained and thoughtful discussion challenging. One of the ways Lee taught her students the skill of engaging in thoughtful discussion about books was by giving them longer periods of time to linger with such books (Short, Harste, & Burke, 1996), while dealing with issues that had importance in their lives (Vasquez, 2014b). To aid in these discussions, she developed a series of engagements for sharing and studying picture books that she called "six sessions for working with a picture book" (see Table 2.1 at the end of the chapter). This strategy helped her students to slow down the process of discussing the connections they were making between the book and their lives. She referred to these sessions as mini-lessons, which she used during readers' or writers' workshop. While discussing the implementation of the six-sessions strategy, Lee noted, "Sometimes I don't go through all six sessions with every book we read together. Sometimes I change the order of the activities or alter them in some way, depending on topics that come up during our conversations." She further commented that the number of days it took to go through the various sessions really depended on the book under study and the issues on hand. Following, she details how she used the six-sessions strategy while working with the book *White Wash* (Shange, 1997).

Six Sessions With White Wash

Session 1: Read Aloud

Choose a book that connects with or represents the students' interests or issues from their lives.

Lee chose *White Wash* to read out loud in response to earlier conversations about how much, or how little, power children have in society. She believed the book extended the idea of students taking action with its message of children working together as a group to protect a classmate. In the past, she had shared with her class books that focused on young people participating in some form of social action. (See Resource Box 2.1 at the end of this chapter for a collection of multimedia text sets in which characters and people take social action.)

> Lee: As I began reading, the class became focused and quiet. When I got to the scene in the book that described the attack, Quinn interrupted, "You tell us not to write violent stories, so how come you're reading us this book with violence in it?"

Quinn was referring to a previous conversation when Lee and the third graders read a series of books on human rights. She had shared two picture books about slavery along with several other titles after which time some of the children chose to focus their narrative writing on some aspect of slavery. Quinn and some other boys had focused on the violence of slavery. Lee suggested to them that their narratives ought to include elements of hope and not to focus solely on violence.

Lee responded to Quinn's comment by stating, "This book has more than violence to it. You'll see what I mean at the end." This incident is a nice demonstration of the ways in which Lee was able to create a space for students to say what is on their minds—an important aspect of being able to build curriculum from the interests of children. It also demonstrates that the children were tuned in to the social messages of the books they were reading.

Session 2: Picture Walk

Session 2 involves revisiting the book for a second time, this time focusing on discussing the storyline of the book as represented by the illustrations.

During this session, Lee had the children work with a partner to fill out a response prompt sheet (see Figure 2.1). She changed the response sheet as needed, to ensure it best suited whatever book they were reading, but in general it contained the same four to six prompts. For example, Lee added, "Why do you think people should or should not read *White Wash*?" to the response prompt sheet for

Why do you think people should or should not read *White Wash*? • It shows that there are some people that do some really bad things. • You should read it because it teaches you to stick up for others. It has kid power in it!	What questions do you have about this story? • If the girl were white, would the Hawks be mean to her? • Why did she stay in her room for so long?
What surprised you about this book? • That the bad people would paint her face white. • I was surprised that they let go of the brother first. • Everything!	Write one or two writing topics from your own life that connect with this story. • My brother is always mean to me and beats me up. • When I got stitches on my chin, I looked like I had a beard. I had to go to school like that. • Being mad
Write one or two statements from someone whose perspective is represented in this book. • (Helene-Angel) I don't want to go outside! They'll bully me again! • (Helene-Angel) I'm hungry, but I can't eat. I hope I can stand up to them next time. • (Brother) I cannot believe I let those boys push my sister around.	Write one or two statements from someone whose perspective is not represented in the book. • (Brother) Run! Leave her alone! • (Gang member) Man, those stupid kids think they can protect her. Ha! • (Gang member) That shows them! It proves white people are better than black people.

FIG. 2.1 Response Prompt Sheet and Some Responses to the *White Wash* Prompt Sheet

..er reflecting on Quinn's comments regarding the vio- . the book. These prompts were statements or questions that .elp the children begin to unpack the book. The children worked with partners to answer the prompts.

Examples of student responses are included in Figure 2.1, which includes some responses to the *White Wash* prompt sheet. Lee then collated the responses on a single sheet of paper for use in subsequent discussions.

Session 3: Small-Group Conversations

In this session, the collated responses are read out loud, after which time the children are sent off for small-group conversation. Sometimes, however, the read-aloud of the responses is followed by a class discussion.

Lee: We read the list of reasons for either reading the book or for censoring the book. Some of the reasons noted by the children for reading *White Wash* were:

- It shows that there are some people that do some really bad things.
- It's a good book.
- It teaches you to stick up for others. It has kid power in it!

As the children reviewed the list, Lee asked them to put a check mark beside any statements that connected in some way to stories they had written previously. Will immediately shared that both books he wrote in class were about sticking up for other people. Robbie noted that his story in which two teenagers escape from being slaves was about kid power.

Next, Lee and her students used writing to think about inequitable ways of being in the world. At every opportunity, she tried to point out the power in writing about important themes and issues from their lives as one way of uncovering how they may have contributed to maintaining inequitable ways of being and as a way to come up with possibilities for disrupting inequities in the world.

After a brief discussion about how readers can benefit from reading *White Wash*, Lee asked her students if they thought the book should be censored and why or why not.

Robbie:	I think the book is violent but not too violent.
Will:	Well it's not . . . I mean it's not like gory and all bloody. They didn't describe it like, "oh look at his bloody arm."
Teacher:	I see. There's a difference?
Will:	It does have some violence but not as much as some other things.
Teacher:	What's something that has a lot of violence, gory violence?
John:	*Scream 2*.
Mark:	*Halloween*.
Tasha:	*Men in Black* has some violence.
Teacher:	So you think the violence in *White Wash* is different than the violence in these movies?

In this exchange, Lee and the children discuss their perspective on violence in terms of violent acts that are not physically gory and gory violence. They use their experience outside of the classroom, drawing from movies they have seen or have heard of, as a resource for making their point. This discussion about violence in books and movies signified to Lee that her students understood the difference between gratuitous violence and the violence used by authors to depict particular scenarios. It also demonstrated to Lee how seamlessly issues from the children's world outside of school could enter into the classroom if space is created for those issues to be explored.

Lee:	In retrospect, I wish I had talked more about this issue of violence, focusing more deeply on differences between violence in the newspaper and violence in movies. Also, I could have discussed in greater detail the impact of reading about violence and using violence in our writing. I've come to accept these moments of 20/20 hindsight as part of a critical literacy curriculum. While I work to become more skillful at guiding critical conversations, I also have a greater awareness that conversations are not scripted entities. They have a life and spirit of their own.

Lee's reflection is a wonderful window into the way she positions herself as a learner—a teacher who engages in ongoing observation and analysis of life in the classroom as a way to best build curriculum that has importance and significance in her students' lives.

After some time, the children were asked to continue their discussion in small groups. Lee had them discuss the list of questions they had about the story from the response sheet (see Figure 2.1). She collated the questions on a sheet of paper and handed out copies to each group. Through the year her students had become very familiar with the process of evaluating questions in terms of how much conversation each generates. The children knew to put a check mark next to questions that did not generate much conversation and a star next to questions that were discussed at length. Lee noticed that this strategy helped her students develop substantive comments for literature circle discussions where small groups of children talk about various topics or issues connected to a particular book they are reading. For example, as Lee's students moved through the list of questions for *White Wash*, one group of three girls and one boy covered a wide range of topics, including racism, the issue of the main character's embarrassment over what has happened to her, the motivation of the gang members, and children protecting one another.

Session 4: Whole-Group Meeting

During session 4, the response list is revisited to deal with the issue(s) raised during session 3.

Brad:	She was embarrassed because they put paint all over her face, and she didn't want to go to school. She might have thought that all the kids . . .
Brenda:	She was afraid.
Kevin:	Like when she walked into school, they'd probably be all laughing.
Teacher:	People might laugh about it?
Kevin:	Yeah.
Lisa:	Well, I think that she might not want to go out because they could have done something a lot worse. They still could do something worse to her.
Will:	Maybe she was just embarrassed because she didn't want to face them [her friends].
John:	Maybe because she let someone paint her face white instead of running away.

Kristen: Like she might be afraid that her friends would be like, you let a white person attack you like that?
Teacher: Do you think her friends would do that?
Kristen: No, but she might think that.
Lisa: She did say, "I'm an embarrassment to the whole race."
Brad: And people might say, "You let people paint your face white? And you're trying to be white?" Because I mean, if they didn't know what happened?
Hank: Maybe if they didn't know how it had happened.
Teacher: Well, her friends did support her.
Quinn: At the end.

According to Lee, the issue of shame came up many times in their discussions.

Lee: It's a difficult issue for me. I tried to focus on the importance of awareness while acknowledging that these topics were emotional and often uncomfortable. There were no easy answers to these questions. While I guided the conversation, I considered myself a participant as we explored issues that troubled all of us. It was clear to me that the kids were ready to talk about the gritty issues in *White Wash*. They were not glossing over the issues in the text but confronting them head on. They were not simply summarizing or merely asking why. They brought in connections from their own lives, the media, other books, and from previous conversations we've had.

Session 5: Choose an Illustration

During session 5, students gather together to choose an illustration from the book to post on the learning wall (Vasquez, 2005a, 2014). (See Resource Box 2.2 at the end of the chapter for more about learning walls.) The learning wall is a large, floor-to-ceiling bulletin board in the classroom that holds important artifacts from the school year—photographs, souvenirs from field trips, newspaper headlines, and more. Each time a social issue picture book is read, an illustration is selected from the book as a reminder of the conversations about it. A caption is created to go along with each of the illustrations. Both are then posted on the learning wall.

Lee: The students were familiar with this activity. I told them to think about which picture was most important as I picture walk through the pages of the book. They talked as they decided which illustration to post and defended their choices along the way. With some books, there was clear consensus among the kids. With others, kids chose a variety of illustrations. If no clear choice emerged, I picked a picture that connected with or highlighted our conversations. The conversations about which picture to choose re-immersed us in the text.

For *White Wash* we selected the picture at the end of the book, in which all Helene-Angel's friends come to her house to escort her to school. Together we composed a caption for the picture. One student typed the caption in a large, colorful font and printed it. Another student mounted the picture and caption on construction paper. The page was laminated and stapled to the learning wall (Vasquez, 1998), which by this time of year was filled with striking illustrations from picture books as well as our own classroom artifacts. To me, it looked like a museum gallery or a giant collage. It helped visitors to our classroom know more about our class curriculum and helped us to reflect on our year together.

Session 6: Notebook Writing

In this session, prompt sheets are returned to the students. They are then asked to expand on, in their writer's notebook, the writing topics they identified in session 2.

The children are to write at least one page on their topic. When most of them appear to be done, the class is asked to meet. Children who are not finished bring their notebooks with them and continue writing as they listen. The children are asked to take turns sharing their writing. Those who are not ready for sharing have the option of passing, but everyone has to at least share his or her topic with the group. The topics may vary with some being more personal and fun while others are more sociological and serious.

Lee's experience was that children frequently wanted to change their writing topic by this time because newer ideas had come up for them since the first few sessions. This happened as they listened to one another and reflected on their initial stances or ideas, through the stances or ideas of their classmates. This also happened as they continued to make connections between the text and their own life experiences. For instance, Brad wrote about people making fun of his last name. Will wrote about face painting at the school carnival. Alice, an Asian American student, wrote about being called "Brownie" and "Blacky" by children at school. Hank wrote about having to take care of his little brother. Meg wrote about her brother having an accident with a can of spray paint in their garage. Brenda wrote about her Sudanese neighbors, exclaiming "I definitely would not paint their face white!" Kevin wrote about the time he was embarrassed to come to school with stitches in his chin. Blaire wrote about a shooting in the New York subway she had heard about on the news: "Why did someone shoot that person?" Upon reflecting on session 6, Lee wrote in her journal,

> Our study of *White Wash* came at the end of the school year. Throughout the year, we had used the six-sessions chart with nearly 20 texts. Most of these were picture books, but we also used the chart to study chapter books and a video about social action. I used the six-sessions chart as a tool for allowing more voices to be heard in classroom conversations and for digging deeper into the real-world issues explored in these texts.

Lingering Thoughts and Ways Forward

In this chapter, Lee made visible the intertextuality of books as she showed how her students drew connections between their own experiences outside of the classroom and their experiences with texts to engage in powerful talk. As new issues emerged, such as violence in writing, the media, and the trauma of being victimized, the third graders extended their understanding of past topics (racism, shame, and social action). Using social issues texts (see Resource Box 2.3 at the end of this chapter) in combination with other texts was a way to bring real-world issues happening outside the classroom into the classroom. Creating opportunities for her students to linger with texts provided them with an opportunity to re-visit the text, make more connections, and use different lenses through which to read those texts, thereby giving them multiple opportunities to revise and refine their thinking regarding various issues, topics and events.

Reflection Questions

This chapter focused on reading critically using children's books, learner's inquiry questions, and issues in the world outside of school. Even though the focus was on reading, the mini-lessons created by Lee and other strategies she used can be readily adapted for use across different content areas.

1. How might the prompt sheet questions be re-designed for use in the science or social studies curriculum?
2. How might a learning wall work to make visible the children's learning/thinking in the content areas?
3. Lee's six sessions blend together strategies for learners to work independently, in small groups, and as a whole group. The sessions also create spaces for the children to read both images and text as they construct meaning for themselves. How might these sessions and strategies work to provide both powerful and pleasurable opportunities for exploring social issues in the content areas?
4. As the children engaged in the sixth session of Lee's strategy, social issues stemming from the children's lives began to emerge. For instance Brad wrote about people making fun of his last name. Alice, an Asian American student, wrote about being called "Brownie" and "Blacky" by children at school. What might Lee have done to create spaces for children to take on these issues, which directly impact the children's lives?

Try This

- Reflect on the various kinds of books you share with your students. From those books, what kinds of social issues or topics do the children have opportunities to discuss?
- Make a list of books or other texts, including multimedia texts such as songs, movies, or websites, through which you could raise social issues. Reflect on your existing curriculum and identify some spaces in which you could use some of these texts to try using Lee's six-session strategy.
- Record a discussion that you have with your students as you engage with a book. What kinds of questions are raised during these discussions? What do you do with the questions raised? How might Lee's strategy for sustaining conversation change the nature of your conversations?

TABLE 2.1
Lee's Six Sessions for Working With a Picture Book

Session Number	Description
Session 1 Read Aloud	Read the book out loud and give students ample time to make connections, comment, and ask questions.
Session 2 Picture Walk	Have students meet in small groups to discuss the book and fill out a response sheet that includes the following prompts: 1. What is important to remember about this book? 2. What surprised you about this book? 3. What questions do you have? 4. Name a possible writing topic from your own life that relates to the book. The teacher then compiles all the students' questions on one sheet.
Session 3 Small-Group Conversations	Gather groups of students to meet and discuss the question list generated from the response sheets. Then groups monitor their responses to the questions by putting a check mark next to questions that did not generate much conversation and a star next to questions that were discussed at length.
Session 4 Whole-Group Meeting	Have the class meet as a whole group to discuss the starred questions.
Session 5 Choose an Illustration	Have the group discuss one illustration from the book that they collectively feel best represents the conversations about it. Once an illustration is selected, it is posted on the learning wall (Vasquez, 1998) along with a caption.
Session 6 Notebook Writing	Ask each student to write a couple of pages in his or her notebook about the writing topics noted on the response sheet during session 2. These entries are later revisited to determine potential topics to develop further.

Resource Box 2.1 Multimedia Text Set in Which Characters and People Take Social Action

I. Picture Books

Cohn, D., & Rodriguez, L.J. (2005). *¡Si se puede! Yes we can!* Madison, WI: Turtleback.

This is a bilingual book about the justice for janitors strike in Los Angeles, California, as told from the perspective of a young boy whose mother becomes a leader of the strike.

Winter, J. (2008). *Wangari's trees of peace: A true story from Africa.* New York: Harcourt Children's Books.

This is a powerful picture book biography that introduces Kenyan environmentalist Wangari Maathai, who won the Nobel Peace Prize in 2004. The story follows the founding of the Green Belt Movement, a movement that advocates for human rights and peaceful democratic change through the protection of the environment.

II. Websites

The Green Belt Movement (http://www.greenbeltmovement.org/)

This website includes images representing the movement as well as videos and resources.

Children Helping Children (http://children-helping-children.com/)

This is a website with video, photo images, and resources regarding the Children Helping Children organization founded by concert violinist Jourdan Urbach with other child prodigies when he was only 7 years old. The organization is a musical charity foundation that fundraises nationally for pediatric divisions of hospitals and medical charity organizations. Proceeds from Jourdan's Carnegie Hall Debut went to benefit The National Multiple Sclerosis Society.

III. Music

Critical Literacy in Practice Podcast, "Save Our School" Clip (http://andybilodeau.com/clip/2006/10/16/save-our-school-_-clip-15/)

This song is performed by a group of kindergarten to grade six children at Selsted Primary School, located in a small rural community in Southeast Kent in the United Kingdom. Selsted was one of 12 schools earmarked for closure because of falling pupil numbers in the county. In protest, the children and adults of the school formed The Save Selsted Action Group, which then wrote a song to protest its proposed closure.

Resource Box 2.2 Resources for Constructing a Learning Wall

Harste, J., Leland, C., Lewison, M., Ociepka, A., & Vasquez, V. (2000). Supporting critical conversations in classrooms. In K. M. Pierce (Ed.), *Adventuring with books* (pp. 507–512). Urbana, IL: National Council of Teachers of English.

Harste, J., & Vasquez, V. (1998). The work we do: Journal as audit trail. *Language Arts*, 75(4), 266–276.

Vasquez, V. (2001a). Creating a critical literacy curriculum with young children. *Phi Delta Kappa International Research Bulletin No. 29*. Bloomington, IN: Phi Delta Kappa.

Vasquez, V. (2001b). Negotiating critical literacies in elementary classrooms. In B. Comber & A. Simpson (Eds.), *Critical literacy at elementary sites* (pp. 55–58). Mahwah, NJ: Erlbaum.

Vasquez, V. (2014). *Negotiating critical literacies with young children*. New York: Routledge.

Resource Box 2.3 What Are Social Issues Texts?

It is important to reemphasize that I use books as only one of many tools for constructing critical literacies, as one of many artifacts for mediating critical literacy work. However, books alone, even those books referred to as social issues texts (Harste, Leland, Lewison, Ociepka, & Vasquez, 2000)—such as texts that address topics of race, class, or gender—are useful as tools to do critical literacy work only insofar as they can be vehicles for discussing issues of power and control. Simply having these books available is not enough. What makes them social issues texts are the differences that the discourses or belief-laden ways of being and talking have on our discussion about those books and the experiences that influence those discussions, along with who is able to participate, in what ways, for what purposes, and to what ends. It is most advantageous to use such books in combination with other texts as a way of helping students to understand that texts are never neutral and that they are constructed for particular reasons and audiences. Using one book and the ideas presented within as a frame through which to read another book provides for a more informed reading than when students are asked to use individual books. Using a combination of multimedia texts (books, songs, everyday texts, etc.) makes for an even more informed reading because this practice relocates meaning making beyond what is gleaned from our experiences with print-based texts—or, more specifically, books—to sociocultural/sociopolitical spaces.

3

Writing to Disrupt Inequities

Curtis:	Who are those again?
Patrick:	Oh, Mounties.
Julia:	When I grow up I can be one!
Roger:	When I grow up I will be a horse.
Emily:	You can't be a horse; you're a person, not an animal!
Curtis:	No, you can't! There are no girl Mounties in the poster.

This conversation took place in a kindergarten classroom I shared with 16 children, all of them 4 or 5 years old. They were referring to a poster of the Royal Canadian Mounted Police (RCMP), which they were using to discuss who could or could not be an RCMP officer. The RCMP, also referred to as Mounties, is Canada's national police force, founded more than 125 years ago to enforce the law during Canada's early settlement days. Today the RCMP acts as the municipal police force in about 200 Canadian cities and towns.

During the year that this discussion took place, the parents of one of the children in the class were RCMP officers. As such, they were able to arrange for another officer to visit the children. After the visit, the officer left a poster of the Mounties' Musical Ride Team on horseback, which he put up on a bulletin board in the classroom. Spectators have described the routine performed by the Musical Ride Team as a ballet on horses. On the poster the team is lined up in a row so the officers' faces are clearly visible. The opening conversation took place as the children began to look more closely at the details of the poster while they worked on their various class projects. Although the children were working on different things (drawing, writing, painting) they joined in conversation with each other and engaged in emergent listening (Rinaldi, 2006), remaining open to what each other had to say. This openness contributed to the emergence of ideas that surfaced through the intra-action between the children, the poster, and the classroom space, where the children had the flexibility to work with materials of their choice, creating opportunities for such encounters to readily unfold. As the classroom teacher I too remained open to the not-yet-known as a way to create space for issues of importance to the children to surface.

The Emergent Curriculum as the Real Curriculum

Manning (1993) talks about three curricula that play out in the classroom: the mandated curriculum, which is provided by the school district head offices; the paper curriculum, which consists of the curriculum guides that are often part of prepackaged programs; and the real curriculum, which refers to the issues and topics raised by students in classrooms. The conversation at the opening of this chapter represents the real curriculum, one that emerged through conversation and one that generated other interests. Anything that students or teachers bring to the classroom has the potential to become the real curriculum. Since what might be brought to the classroom cannot be pre-determined, said curriculum is one that is emergent. This curriculum and what children learn from it in terms of skills and content often intersect with the paper and mandated curriculum even though this intersecting is not pre-planned. It simply looks and sounds different as it is negotiated and shaped in conversation and through listening closely and openly to what children are saying and where their interests may lie.

As the classroom teacher, I took it upon myself to keep track of ways in which this real curriculum complemented or connected with what was required by the school board. What makes the real curriculum sound and look different are the different ways of talking that are brought to bear on the issues raised by children. These different ways of talking, or discourses, provide alternate frameworks through which children can speak about and make meaning in the world around them, using various resources and materials of their choice.

In this chapter, the focus is on student writing and the kind of written work that children produce while taking up social issues that emerge through working with everyday texts, children's books, and various materials in the classroom. It is also about what happens when alternate discourses (Gee, 2005), or ways of being, doing, and talking, are used to engage in open and critical discussion about these texts. According to Haas Dyson (2005), everyday texts are as follows:

- Texts that are spoken or written as part of everyday life.
- Texts that are so common that we don't carefully take notice of them.

We are less aware of the kinds of messages about our world that are conveyed by everyday texts. Because these are not natural representations of the world, they can be deconstructed and analyzed to uncover the view of the world they represent to make visible the lifestyles and identities that are constructed through what is presented and through how it is presented. See Resource Box 3.1 to learn more about everyday texts.

You Can Be a Mountie When You Grow Up

Jessica: There's no girls. There's no girls in it.
Roger: There's men.
Nicholas: 'Cause there's horses.
Teacher: Let's talk about that for a minute. A lot of you have been saying there are no girls in it. What does that tell you? What does this poster say about being a girl Mountie?
Andrea: Well, um, one time my dad went up a mountain and there was only girls in it. There was no boys.
Teacher: Oh, really. So there was another—so in that case there were only girls and no boys. Is that what you're saying?
Patrick: Because there's boys and men and there's no girls because um, girls are not like boys are they?

Teacher: So do you mean that you don't think they can do this job? That being a Mountie is a boy thing to do? Does anyone have anything they'd like to say about that?
Girls: Yeah!
Jessica: Well, my dad. He lets me ride on his back when he's pretending to be a horse to try and catch my brother Kyle. Well, since I know something like I go on my merry-go-round at Woodbine and at Square One [shopping malls], that it tells me that I could go on it too 'cause I know how to ride like girls 'cause both feet on one side and then you ride. But on real horses you gotta hold tight and do the same.
Kyle: Um, I went on the merry-go-round at Square One and that tells me that um, um, that I like horses and I ride one horse but not with these men on it. I didn't wear the hat like that or the coats.
Andrea: One time I went on a real horse. My daddy helped me. When I went on the horse I was just 3 years old and I—it was the sister. When she was 4 years old she fell in front of her horsey.
Jessica: Well, girls, they can take boys' place even if they don't know how to hammer and all that 'cause my mom, dad he works with wood down in the basement to finish it and mom she helps and I'm a girl right? So I help, too. Well, once dad I think was sick, but he didn't tell me the rest 'cause I don't think he was feeling well when he didn't tell me the rest. 'Cause a girl took his place, and he had to get off work 'cause he was starting to bleed or he was sick to get off work.
Teacher: And a girl took his place?
Jessica: Yeah.
Teacher: What do you think about that?
Jessica: I think that girls could ride horses too!

The Mountie poster, which began a class conversation about how girls/females are constructed by social text, represents one way in which males are privileged in society. If the previous conversation had not taken place, it is possible that this poster would have remained, implicitly stabilizing an inequitable distribution of power between males and females.

The comments made by Andrea, "Well, um, one time my dad went up a mountain and there was only girls in it. There was no boys," and Patrick, "Because there's boys and men and there's no girls because um, girls are not like boys are they?" begin to tease at the students' perception of how boys and girls, and men and women, are positioned by everyday texts such as the poster. Andrea cites an example of an all-girls situation to counter the all-boys Mountie poster. Patrick makes a statement that girls are not like boys, implicitly reasoning that there are no girls in the poster because girls are not like boys. Patrick's statement could lead to the conclusion that girls are not capable of being Mounties because there is something they cannot do that boys are able to do.

As the conversation continues, making problematic the absence of women in the poster, traditional notions of femininity are challenged and traditional male and female roles destabilized. Jessica begins to construct her model of possibility for girls and women as she draws from her personal experience of riding horses: "I know something like I go on my merry-go-round at Woodbine and at Square One, that it tells me that I could go on it too 'cause I know how to ride like girls 'cause both feet on one side and then you ride." Here Jessica builds a claim for her argument that girls can ride horses too by drawing on her own experiences—her embodied knowledge. Although, in building her claim, she draws on a stereotype of girls riding side-saddle, she quickly uproots the stereotype when she says, "but on real horses you gotta hold tight and do the same." She demonstrates what she means by 'the same,' pointing at the poster and mimicking the riders on the poster. In other words, girls can also ride on the real horses and ride the same way as the Mountie riders. This is Jessica's way of problematizing the absence of females in the poster. She implicitly argues that girls can ride horses and, therefore, should have been represented in the poster. Jessica makes her stance explicit, refuting the poster when she declares, "I think that girls could ride horses too!" meaning that females, therefore, also can be Mounties and should be represented in the poster.

In response to this conversation, the children and I searched through our school library for information about the Mounties. One book that the children were most interested in because of the clear, bold illustrations was *The Royal Canadian Mounted Police*, written and illustrated by Marc Tetro (1994). The cover of the book depicts a group of five Mounties—some short, others tall, all of them sporting mustaches, all of them male. Immediately, comments were made by both boys and girls in the class regarding this book cover being "just the same" as the poster—they both "mean the same" and "tell us the same." One of the girls asked, "Why?"—meaning, why do the book cover and poster both exclude women?

While reading the book, another illustration caught the group's attention. The illustration clearly depicted why the Mountie poster was designed as it was—depicting an all-male police force. The text read, "Among the recruits [RCMP recruits] there were teachers and farmers, students and lumberjacks." All the recruits were male. Some of the children were puzzled by what the text meant but made connections to the poster while looking closely at the illustration. One of the children decided that the person in front must be the farmer because "he is wearing overalls." Someone else decided that a person in the back row must be the student because "the bag he is carrying looks like a backpack." They couldn't decide on which character the lumberjack could be because "what does a lumberjack look like anyway?" They also could not figure out which character the teacher could be because none of them "look like Ms. Vasquez." It was interesting to see the children use their previous experiences, their available cultural capital and ways of being (discourses) that were familiar to them, and what they understood to be the embodiment of people working at particular jobs to construct meaning from the illustrations.

As I continued reading the book, I watched as Andrea and Jessica moved closer to me. "Wait, wait, wait . . . It's the same again, it's all men and no girls." Women had no part in the history of the RCMP as represented by Tetro's book. I asked them to consider what could have been given to women and girls as responsibilities during the times when the Mounties were first created. We looked at some reference books of that time period to see if men were given all the jobs that people thought were important. The children shared examples of women they know who are doctors or lawyers, citing that "Ms. Vasquez is a teacher and she's a girl so it's not exactly the same as before." They were learning that history is a social construction, that previous ways of being can be changed, and that as we live our lives we are in fact writing history, as it emerges from moment to moment.

Picking up on this comment, I shared that there are more jobs taken by women in recent years that have not been available to them in the past. I also shared that this change took a long time and that many women over the years worked hard at making sure that women today have different opportunities. I told them about Emily Stowe, who fought for the rights of women to be admitted to medical school in the 1800s, and Clara Martin, who fought for the rights of women to enter the legal profession. My students and I also talked about how historical constructions, as in the case of the Mounties originally being an all-male group, can easily be maintained and how that might happen. Further discussion took place regarding the need to continue to find ways to make sure that men and women are treated equitably and that women and girls are given the same kinds of opportunities, rights, and privileges that men are given. Jessica interjected with "and this poster and this book does not make things equal." This comment led to a conversation regarding the need to look critically at the way women and girls are represented in different texts like the poster.

As a class we read other books that presented different ways of being (different positionings) for females. Some of the books included *Mama Is a Miner* (Lyon, 1994), *The Paper Bag Princess* (Munsch, 1988), and *Princess Smartypants* (Cole, 1997). We also read and discussed books in which females were marginalized, such as *Counting on Frank* (Clement, 1991) and *Piggybook* (Browne, 1990). All of these books gave us a perspective from which to read magazine fliers and other everyday texts, such as food packaging and toy packaging, and to watch television shows. Recently, many more books have been published that focus on presenting strong female characters. These include books such as *Grace for President* (Dipuchio, 2008), *Julia Morgan Built a Castle* (Mannis, 2006), *Meggie Moon* (Baguley, 2005), *Of Numbers and Stars: The Story of Hypatia* (Love, 2006), and *Sally Jean, the Bicycle Queen* (Best, 2006).

My students and I also talked about doing what we could to help change the way certain groups, such as females, are positioned in society. In response to our conversations, Andrea—whose parents are both in the RCMP—spoke up saying that if they (Mounties) "keep sending this poster out then some people, like girls, won't know that they can be Mounties too."

As our conversation continued, it became clear that, historically, various texts have worked in favor of boys and men. Our conversation implicitly became a way of countering this historical effect and finding ways to have text work differently for girls and women.

A strategy for extending this conversation is to look through the books you have available in the classroom and list the various roles given to male and female characters. This kind of activity creates space to discuss with children alternate ways of being by having them imagine or rewrite some of the stories to create alternate realities. Resource Box 3.2 provides a list of books that can be used to discuss gender issues.

Constructing Alternate Realities

Of all the students in the class, Jessica seemed most eager to take action against the inequities discussed in the classroom. She decided that she needed to show the Mounties what the poster should look like today, "because today, women are Mounties also." In other words, women should not only be given the opportunity to become RCMP but, in fact, they already are in position as RCMP officers; therefore, their presence should be recognized. She called her poster "My Poster of the Way the Mountie Poster Should Be" (see Figure 3.1). In Jessica's poster there is an equitable number of men and women represented. Once completed, she asked me to help her with a letter to the Mounties (see Figure 3.2). Jessica decided to send both the letter and the poster to the RCMP office in the city where she lived.

A few weeks after having posted Jessica's letter and poster, the father of one of the children in another class asked if someone from my class had sent a letter to the RCMP. He then proceeded to

FIG. 3.1 My Poster of How the Mounties Should Be

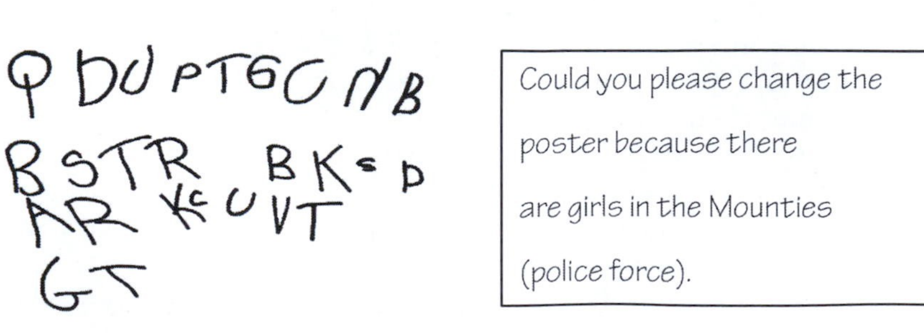

FIG. 3.2 A Letter to the Mounties

share that no one had ever pointed out the inequity in the poster before. When I asked what action would be taken as a result of Jessica's letter, he replied by saying that if those in charge of media promotions do not do anything to resolve this issue that the women in his department certainly would. This Mountie story became a metaphor for the way in which my students and I critically read different texts in our classroom. This included everyday texts such as the Mountie poster and books written for children along with other multimodal texts. No longer did the children read blindly, accepting how texts construct and position them; they began to realize how text could be reconstructed in more equitable ways not only for boys and girls and men and women, but also for people or groups who have been marginalized, disadvantaged, or discriminated against.

Writing Out: Using Writing to Read Critically

Similar to my kindergarten students, after reading Toni and Slade Morrison's (Morrison & Morrison, 1999) *The Big Box*, Janice Shear's fifth-grade gifted students in Mississauga, Ontario, Canada, expressed concern over the issues that emerged through their conversation about the book.

The book has a haunting message about children who fall outside socially accepted norms. In poetic form, the authors tell the stories of Patty, Mickey, and Lisa Sue, who live in a big brown box with doors that open only one way. The adults responsible for these children felt that their behavior required they be locked away because they are unable to handle their freedom. While reflecting on her students' initial reaction to the book, Janice wrote,

> As I closed the book there was an audible sigh from the class. The kids, blinking at each other as if newly awakened from a dream, started some quiet talk, which quickly picked up momentum. The spell had been broken, reality reentered, ideas surfaced. They talked among themselves and repeatedly chanted a line from the book, "They just can't handle their freedom."
>
> They asked me to read the book again. This time they anticipated my reading of the line, chanting repeatedly as I read on.

After first reading *The Big Box* aloud to her class, Janice described what she referred to as her students' seeming delight with the line "they just can't handle their freedom" as problematic. She felt that they did not take the book seriously, nor did they respect the issue at hand. Nevertheless, Janice persisted in discussing the book further, and when they did the tone of the children's conversation changed.

> Janice: After the second reading of the book, [the students] were really upset as to why the characters were placed in the big box. They expressed feelings of anger at the parents and other adults who were responsible and were genuinely puzzled as to what regarding the children's behaviors led their parents to believe that they couldn't handle their freedom. They expressed concern with some adults and institutions that do not allow people to be themselves but realized that when someone is different they are sometimes picked on and in a sense "boxed."

The notion of being "boxed" or "othered" led Janice's students to consider what boxes meant in their own lives. They made statements such as "The box is a place to put a problem so you don't have to deal with it" and "It is a mental [in your head] place rather than a physical place." The box they most identified with was being misunderstood by other students or by adults. To make further sense of their discussions, Janice asked her students to write in their journals about their thoughts regarding the book and the notion of being boxed. These were reflective pieces that were informally written with the intent of providing a space for the children to articulate their thinking and their feeling. Another strategy for helping children to articulate their thinking is "3 Plusses and a Wish" (Burke, 1997), whereby students are asked to write about three things they connected with in the text and one question that came to mind as they read the text or one wish for how they might have wanted the text to unfold. "What's on Your Mind?" is another strategy developed by Burke (1997). With this strategy, students are asked to comment in general or specifically about the text and pose comments, connections, or questions that came to mind as they read the text. "Reading With a Post-It" is another useful strategy that I have seen used by Rise Paynter in her fifth-grade classroom in Bloomington, Indiana. Rise had her students jot down words or ideas on sticky notes, which they then affixed to the pages of the text they were reading. The children would then return to these sticky notes when discussing the texts with their classmates or during class discussion.

Janice's students commented that writing their thoughts helped them to organize their thinking about the text. It seemed writing was a way for Janice's students to think critically about *The Big Box*. While talking about his writing, Kyle described the box as a mental prison. He said,

> It doesn't really exist. The parents made the big box up to trap the kids. And if it was real, it works like a playpen. It traps the kids inside, but the parents, teachers, etc., have complete access to them.

Liane connected with being boxed in as a result of being labeled as gifted. She reflected.

> The other time I've been in a box was when my old friends officially knew I was gifted and they made something up called Liane Carrabanna. They said this character went to St. Rose and they hated her. It was very weird because they were always telling me about her, so I suspected something. I knew it was me. I was right. It was me. It was OK at first, but then I asked them why. They said they did it because I was too smart for them. I think the one way everyone puts everyone else in a box is when we don't give them chances and choices.

Katherine connected to having been boxed in as a result of being female:

> I've been put in a box a couple of times in my life, like when I get grounded. When people (especially boys my age or a bit older) say I'm substitute in a soccer game, or I'm sitting on the bench for the whole game because I'm "only a girl" because they (the team) don't need a girl.

After listening to her students' responses and reflecting on her own journal entries, Janice revisited her concern regarding their initial reaction to the book. She noted that they may have responded the way they did (chanting "they just can't handle their freedom" in a way that made Janice think they were not taking the book seriously) to offset their discomfort and to "offset the intensity of their reactions."

Until Janice talked further with her students, she had not sidered the multiplicity of issues regarding gender equity, fairn and social justice that had emerged for her students. Before creati a space for open conversation she had no idea her students wer mulling over all these issues in their minds while she read the book. It was not until she read their writing and listened to their responses that she began to recognize these issues as important ones to take up in the classroom. Janice was not prepared for how her students reacted to tensions that were clearly new to them. However, she realized that reading and responding critically could not be a one-time experience. As she dealt with the social issues that began to surface she noticed other issues beginning to emerge. For example, in Katherine's writing about *The Big Box,* it became clear to Janice that gender equity was an issue that she ought to take up in the classroom. What Janice cited as an important lesson she learned here, is that there is no one-size-fits-all critical literacy, and that teachers and students together need to construct different critical literacies, depending on what work needs to be done in certain places, settings, contexts, or communities, and that it needs to be negotiated, beginning with using the cultural and linguistic resources of the children.

Engaging in Transformative Writing

Morrell (2008) reminds us that in order to liberate the self or other we need the use of tools or language in order to counter dominant texts that serve the interests of power that privilege some while marginalizing others. Although Morrell's work focuses on adolescent learners, I believe the same principles apply here, where my kindergarten students and Shear's fifth graders engaged in critical discussions of text and used writing as a tool for making sense of the world around them or imagining that things could be other than what they were currently. These can be seen as the beginnings of critical textual production (Enciso, 2011; Morrell, 2008; Tate, 2011), described by Morrell (2008) as texts that "serve as the manifestation of an alternate reality or a not-yet-realized present that only enters into the imagination through the interaction with new and authentically liberating words that are created by writers as cultural workers" (p. 115). In the case of Jessica, her re-designed poster represents an alternate reality for the Mountie's Musical Ride team and therefore female Mounties. For Janice Shear, her students' journal writing resulted in the manifestation of not-yet-realized social inequalities they had experienced in their lives making visible for her issues of importance in their lives from which she could build socially relevant curriculum. No story starter could have produced the kind of thinking and understanding experienced by these young learners. As noted by Tate (2011), through writing these children participated as analysts of their world and/or as producers and creators of different worlds or ways of being. In the end students and teachers alike came to realize the potential of critical writing to contribute to a more just world.

Reflection Questions

1. Keep track of the different ways that your students engage in writing throughout an entire school day. The following chart might be useful for reflecting on the literacies produced and the real-world effects of the writing that you do with your students.

Type of Writing	Purpose/ Intent	Literacies Produced	Real World Effects

2. After filling in the chart in #1, reflect on what differences the various 'writing' your students have done has made in their lives. Which writing was most impactful and in what ways? For whom did particular writing matter and in what ways? What difference might it make for your students to engage in writing from a critical literacy perspective?

Try This

With your students, brainstorm a list of things that matter—that is, issues or topics that are important to the group. You could do this as a whole group, keeping track of the children's comments on a large sheet of chart paper. You could also have each student create their own Important Ideas, Topics and Questions booklet. You can do this by creating a stapleless book (such as the one located at http://www.readwritethink.org/classroom-resources/student-interactives/stapleless-book-30010.html).

Use the list to reflect on the topics or issues from which you create curriculum. Are the things that matter to your students reflected in your paper curriculum? In what ways might you be able to keep your students' interests at the center of your teaching by negotiating the things that matter to them as curriculum?

Resource Box 3.1 Resources to Learn More About Everyday Texts

Alvermann, D. E., Moon, J. S., & Hagood, M. C. (1999). *Popular culture in the classroom: Teaching and researching critical media literacy*. Newark, DE: International Reading Association; Chicago: National Reading Conference.
Barton, D., & Hamilton, M. (1998). *Local literacies: Reading and writing in one community*. London: Routledge.
Comber, B., Nixon, H., & Reid, J. (2007). (Eds.). *Literacies in place: Teaching environmental communications*. Newtown, NSW, Australia: Primary English Teaching Association.
Comber, B., & Thomson, P. (with Wells, M.). (2001). Critical literacy finds a "place": Writing and social action in a low-income Australian grade 2/3 classroom. *The Elementary School Journal*, 101(4), 451–464.
Marsh, J. (2005). (Ed.). *Popular culture, new media and digital literacy in early childhood*. New York: Routledge Falmer.
O'Brien, J. (1994). Show Mum you love her: Taking a new look at junk mail. *Reading*, 28(1), 43–46.
Vasquez, V. (2000). Building community through social action. *School Talk*, 5(4), 2–3.
Vasquez, V. (2003). What Pokemon can teach us about learning and literacy. *Language Arts*, 81(2), 118–125.
Vasquez, V. (2004). *Negotiating critical literacies with young children*. Mahwah, NJ: Erlbaum.
Vasquez, V. (2007, May). Using the everyday to engage in critical literacies with young children. *New England Reading Association Journal*, 43(2), 6–11.
Vasquez, V., & Egawa, K. (Eds.). (2002). Everyday texts, everyday literacies. *School Talk*, 8(1), 1–8.

Resource Box 3.2 Children's Books That Can Be Used to Discuss Gender Issues

The best beekeeper of Lalibela: A tale from Africa. New York: Holiday House.
Breen, S. (2008). *Violet the pilot*. New York: Penguin/Dial Books for Young Readers.
Browne, A. (1986). *Piggybook*. New York: Knopf.

Buehner, C. (1996). *Fanny's dream*. New York: Dial.
Clement, R. (1991). *Counting on Frank*. Milwaukee, WI: Gareth Stevens.
Cole, B. (1997). *Princess Smartypants*. New York: Putnam.
dePaola, T. (1979). *Oliver Button is a sissy*. San Diego, CA: Harcourt Brace.
Henson, H. (2008). *That book woman*. New York: Simon & Schuster.
Hoffman, M. (1991). *Amazing Grace*. New York: Dial.
Hopkinson, D. (2001). *Under the quilt of night*. New York: Atheneum.
Fitzgerald, D. (2005). *Getting in the game*. New York: Roaring Brook.
Karr, K. (2005). *Mama went to jail for the vote*. New York: Hyperion Books for Children.
Kessler, C. (2000). *My great-grandmother's gourd*. New York: Orchard.
Lipp, F. (2001). *The caged birds of Phnom Penh*. New York: Holiday House.
Lipp, F. (2008). *Running shoes*. Watertown, MA: Charlesbridge.
Lyon, G. (1994). *Mama is a miner*. New York: Scholastic.
Mackall, D. D. (2008). *A girl named Dan*. Farmington Hills, MI: Sleeping Bear.
Maury, I. (1976). *My mother the mail carrier/Mi mamá la cartera*. New York: Feminist Press.
McCully, E. A. (1996). *The bobbin girl*. New York: Dial.
McCully, E. A. (2000). *Mirette & Bellini cross Niagara Falls*. New York: Putnam.
Miller, W. (1994). *Zora Hurston and the chinaberry tree*. New York: Lee & Low.
Munsch, R. (1986). *The paper bag princess*. Toronto, ON: Annick.
Pinkney, A. D. (2000). *Let it shine: Stories of black women freedom fighters*. San Diego, CA: Harcourt.
Pinkney, A. D. (2003). *Fishing day*. New York: Hyperion.
Schroeder, A. (2000). *Minty: A story of young Harriet Tubman*. New York: Puffin.
Sills, L. (2005). *From rags to riches: A history of girls' clothing in America*. New York: Holiday House.
Yolen, J. (2002). *Hippolyta and the curse of the Amazons*. New York: HarperCollins.
Zipes, J. (Ed.). (1989). *Don't bet on the prince: Contemporary feminist fairy tales in North America and England*. New York: Routledge Kegan & Paul.
Zolotow, C. (1972). *William's doll*. New York: Harper & Row.

4

Critical Literacy and Mathematics Investigations

Teacher: You're not excited about the choices I mentioned this morning? (museum, zoo)

Malcolm: No. We've done those before. It's the same thing every year.

Teacher: Hm. I guess I never thought about it that way. Do you have any suggestions about where we might go?

Malcolm: I just think we should do something fun like a pool party or something.

Teacher: Well, I'm pretty sure that because of rules the school board has in place that we can't do a pool party. They have concerns about students and safety.

Georgia: Well, what if we didn't leave and had a day where we had a dance and pizza and then a party here in the room.

Teacher: OK. That's an idea. Are there any others?
Malcolm: I think we should go to Canada's Wonderland (amusement theme park).
Class: Yeah! That's a great idea!

Michael Muise had just begun to explore opportunities for critical literacy with his fifth- and sixth-grade students when the previous conversation took place regarding an end-of-the-year class excursion. Mike's multiage classroom was in an urban elementary school in Toronto, Ontario, Canada. In this chapter you become privy to the ways in which Mike and his students attempted to understand particular school institutional discourses to find the best way to advance their agenda of planning an alternative end-of-the-year celebration. I share his use of children's literature and math investigations specifically as a way of creating space to encourage the critical reading of social practices in his classroom. Social practices are "particular ways of doing and being, as well as particular ways of acting and talking that are rooted in life experiences" (Vasquez, Egawa, Harste, & Thompson, 2004, p. xi). Further, "since different people have different life experiences it follows that social practices are differentially available to various individuals and groups of people" (p. xi). What this means is not everyone has equitable or equal access to literacy or other opportunities.

Creating a Democratic Learning Environment

In his journal Mike wrote the following:

> Sarah Perry's (1995) book *If*. . . entices readers to imagine what if . . . What if worms had wheels? What if spiders could read Braille? What if hummingbirds told secrets? Her book bends the imagination in much the same way a thick piece of glass refracts light, causing one's eyes to see something from a different perspective. I decided to read the book to my fifth and sixth graders. My intent was to use it as a way to generate writing and to inject some creativity and interest in my writing program. I envisioned it to be a way of stretching and pulling at my students' imagination. In the midst of a class discussion about the book, Malcolm asked, "What if we got to pick where we went for our end-of-the-year trip?"

> I recall trying to reason with my 3-year-old son, Avery, one evening around bath time. I informed him that he had three choices: (1) Get in the tub, (2) Get in bed, or (3) Get your mother. He responded, "But daddy, those aren't my choices. Those are yours." Malcolm, like Avery, was letting me know that my choices were just that—my choices. None of which were my students' choices. Clearly, my ideas for a school excursion were not what Malcolm or his classmates had in mind.

It was early May, and Mike and his students had been talking in class about where they might go for their end-of-the-year outing. He had provided his students with a number of choices, including places other classes had visited in the past. The concept of choice, however, was not always clear to him.

Malcolm: Are all school trips supposed to be no fun?
Teacher: Well, not exactly, but we do need to let your parents and Mr. Morely [the school principal] know that our trip is tied to what we learned here in class.

Picking up on the what-if theme in the book they had been reading, Mike put forth the question, What if we were to think about our school trip from a mathematics perspective? J.J. responded, "Yeah. We could count the number of people in line-ups, and how much it costs for lunch, and . . . " It was then that Mike realized how he and his students might be able to use their proposed trip to Canada's Wonderland as a way to show administration and parents how much learning happens in everyday contexts and, in their case specifically, how mathematics is used in the world outside of the classroom.

Mike: Perry's book *If* . . . led to conversations that helped me to realize the choices I had been providing my students, although well intentioned, were in fact not their choices at all. Conversation about the book provided a forum for my students to examine everyday school practices such as the policy involved with approving or disapproving school events. In addition, discussion of texts such as *If* . . . afforded me an opportunity to critically examine my teaching practices.

Mike and his students had predicted that if they could connect the paper curriculum—in particular, the math curriculum that was mandated by the school board—to their proposed school trip to Canada's Wonderland, they would have a better chance of getting their trip approved by the school's administration. To do this, Mike implemented the use of math investigation journals (Schmidt, 1998; Whitin & Whitin, 2004). These were notebooks specifically used to write and think about mathematics-related topics, inquiry questions, and issues. They served as a tool for children to help sort through concepts they know or wish to know regarding mathematics. In their book *Math Is Language Too: Talking and Writing in the Mathematics Classroom*, Whitin and Whitin (2000) describe the use of math journals as a tool for children to talk, write, and reason about topics, issues, and concepts in relation to mathematics. They note that when children do this kind of journaling, they are able to move beyond the right answer to engage in a metacognitive exploration of what is going on as they problem solve.

Mike and his students used the journal entries to develop topics for investigation and subsequently to use their discoveries and their new learning, in other situations. The process begins with a student selecting a topic of interest. His students were interested in demonstrating to their parents and the school administrators the academic viability of a trip to Canada's Wonderland. In order to do this, prior to beginning their research, Mike had his students map out a plan for their investigation and identify the resources they would be using.

Counting on Frank: *Using Math Journals*

To get the math investigations started, Mike decided to read to the class *Counting on Frank* (Clement, 1991). In this story, Frank, an inquisitive young boy, finds many uses for his talent of counting. He reveals an uncanny ability to use mathematics to estimate, hypothesize, and theorize about the world around him:

> My dad says, "You have a brain. Use it!" So I do. I sit down and fill my notebook with facts. Did you know that the average ballpoint pen draws a line 7,000 feet long before the ink runs out? My

> parents consider this fact to be a bit childish, but I'm sure the pen company would like to know.
>
> (n.p.)

Mike used the book to set up a discussion for his students to identify math unfolding in the world. Other books that create similar kinds of spaces include *If the World Were a Village: A Book About the World's People* (Smith, 2002) and *One Hen: How One Small Loan Made a Big Difference* (Smith Milway, 2008). *If the World Were a Village* asks readers to imagine the whole world as a village of just 100 people. Using 100 people, Smith addresses a number of different social issues and topics such as illiteracy and languages of power, statistically breaking down how each topic or issue plays out across the globe. Notions of power, control, access, and dominance that come to mind while reading the various statistics create a space for children to develop a different way of reading the world, thereby providing an opportunity for them to understand their own privileges and disadvantages. *One Hen* is inspired by true events. The central character is Kojo, a boy from Ghana, who after the death of his father has to quit school to help his mother collect firewood to sell at the market. With a small loan from the village families, Kojo buys a hen. One year later, he has built up a flock of 25 hens. Using his earnings, he is able to return to school while maintaining his farm, which grows to become the largest in the region. Included in the book is an exploration of microloans and resources for children to explore. Microloan is a lending system for people in developing countries who have no collateral and no access to conventional banking.

A strategy that would work well using the books previously mentioned, especially in terms of raising awareness regarding the many ways that each of us can contribute to changing inequitable ways of being in the world, is a strategy developed by Whitin and Whitin (2004) that they refer to as "book pairs." With book pairs, math-related books are used in combination to help children connect math ideas to their everyday world. This is consistent with Short, Harste, and Burke's (1996) observation that when texts are read in combination, an opportunity is created for children to "extend their understandings of each text differently than if only one text had been read" (p. 537). Each book in the pairing offers students a mathematical lens through which to read the world around them. As part of this strategy, students are given the option of creating their own nonfiction texts based on math-related issues of importance to them while borrowing from the formats of the book pairs they have read.

Mike realized the potential of using books in this way and of taking up other social issues, such as gender inequity, with books like *Counting on Frank* and the other books previously noted. He also realized how literature could be used as a powerful tool for helping his students name the stories and issues of importance in their own lives. This is in keeping with Christensen's (2000) notion that part of our work as teachers should be to help make visible for our students those things that have been so much a part of their lives that they are taken for granted or ignored. For the time being, however, Mike decided to focus on the Canada's Wonderland project. He asked his students to brainstorm ways in which they thought mathematics was being used in different areas of the theme park. This initiating experience led his students to generate some ideas about where and how mathematics was used in the daily functioning and operation of Canada's Wonderland. Each student was then provided with a math investigation journal in which to record thoughts, findings, comments, and questions. (See Figure 4.1 for examples of the children's work.)

In his journal, Mike wrote,

> I witnessed my students engaged in learning at many levels. Many logged onto the computer searching for websites that could inform their research. Some discovered the role of angles, measurement, time, and velocity in the construction of park rides such as roller coasters. Other students buried themselves in the library, seeking out books that explored other theme parks around the world, trying to gather data on such things as park capacities, ride capacities, and group discounts. Others looked at maps of Toronto to identify the quickest and most cost efficient route to Wonderland from our school.
>
> Our classroom engagements around their goal of going to Canada's Wonderland lasted approximately two weeks. As a culminating experience, the students agreed that a letter to the school principal would be appropriate. It was discussed that before we sought permission from parents we should get approval from the school. With this in mind, each student was asked to draft a letter demonstrating what he or she had learned with regard to mathematical uses at an amusement park.

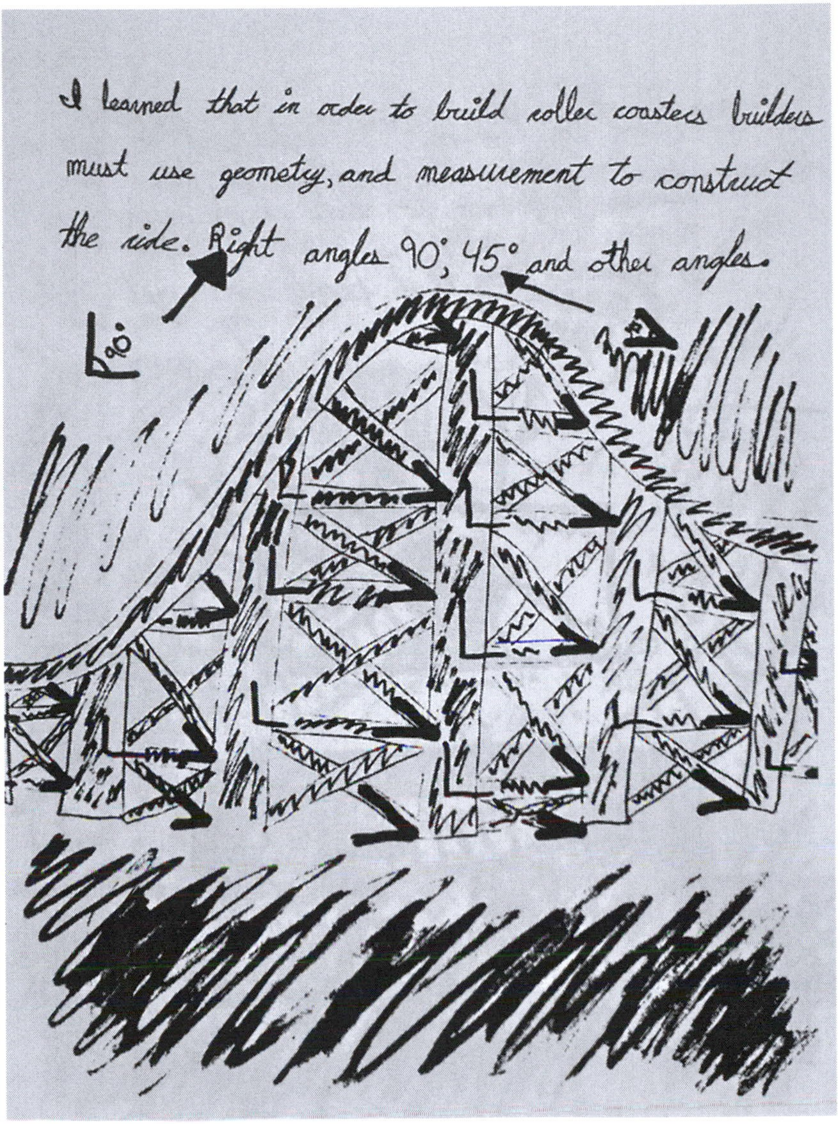

FIG. 4.1A Examples of Students' Work in Their Math Journals

In order for Canada's Wonderland to run as a business they have to take people's money. Money is used so that people can get into the park, buy food and even play games.
$10.00
Canada
Canada
Enter

FIG. 4.1B

Velocity is a calculation that tells the speed of the rides. I learned that different rides need to go different speeds so that people won't fall out and get hurt.
Weeee eee!

FIG. 4.1C

Throughout the following week, the students engaged in formulating a class letter that accompanied their individual letters.

> Dear Mr. Morley,
>
> For the past several weeks, Mr. Muise's class has been working very hard to demonstrate to you and the parents that a class trip to Canada's Wonderland would not only be a tremendous amount of fun but also would be a very good educational experience.
>
> In order to support our argument, we decided to explore the many uses of mathematics within the everyday operations of Canada's Wonderland. In our research, which lasted more than two weeks, we discovered that in order for this park to function they have to make use of geometry, currency, time, fractions, division, multiplication, addition, subtraction, probability, velocity, problem solving, and measurement. These are all areas of math that we have looked at this year and in the past.
>
> We feel that we have worked very hard to find several reasons why this trip would be educational. Please consider our trip to Canada's Wonderland. It is something that we all want very badly. We have attached a few of our math investigation journals for you to look at. We hope you will see that we have done a lot of work to show you that this trip would be both educational and safe. We think it would be a lot of fun too.
>
> Sincerely,
>
> Mr. Muise's Grade 5–6 Students

The letter was submitted to the school's principal on a Tuesday afternoon. On Wednesday morning before the children arrived at school, Mike was called into Mr. Morley's office. Mr. Morley wanted to know what the letter was all about. Mike informed him that he had provided the children with the opportunity to choose where they would go for their end-of-year excursion and that the class unanimously decided on a visit to Canada's Wonderland. He reassured the principal that he understood his concerns and shared with him the children's research on the educational value of such a trip.

> Mike: I asked him if he had read the letter and the math investigation journals the kids had completed. He responded that he, in fact, had looked them over and, while he did find them to be most impressive he was unsure how the school board would feel about a group of 10- to 12-year olds going to an amusement park. He informed me that in all likelihood he would have to say no to the class's proposal. I asked him how he planned to let them know that their efforts were fruitless. He asked if I would let them know. I responded by asking him to come to the class and let them know himself. We compromised with a letter from his office.

In his letter to Mike's students, Mr. Morley wrote,

> Dear Mr. Muise's Grade 5–6 Students,
>
> I want to thank you for your letter requesting permission to go to Canada's Wonderland for your end-of-the-school-year trip. It is clear to me that you all have done a tremendous amount of work. I am impressed that you have found so many practical uses for mathematics within the everyday workings of Canada's Wonderland. However, it is unlikely that such a trip would receive school board approval. There are guidelines and regulations that teachers and principals must abide by when considering places to visit for school outings. My main concern arises around the theme park's water rides. There are very strict rules about students participating in any engagements outside of school that involve water. I am sure you will understand that this decision was not an easy one. I appreciate your incredible work efforts.
>
> Sincerely,
>
> Mr. Morley

It should come as no surprise that Mike's class was disappointed. As he read the letter to them, their shoulders fell and their faces expressed disappointment. Numerous sighs and moans could be heard. Malcolm, however, spoke up and asked, "Who makes the rules for teachers anyway?" Mike told him that many people are involved in creating the rules that are meant to ensure students' time in school is safe and educational. He alluded, however, to the school board as being the primary constructors of such rules. Malcolm then asked who could be contacted at the school board so that he and some others from the class could show how much work had been done in preparation for the proposed trip. Mike told his students that if they wanted to contact someone, the superintendent would be the next logical person. With Malcolm's encouragement, the class decided that a letter should be sent to the superintendent asking for his permission to go to Canada's Wonderland. Over the course of the next few days, the students drafted, edited, revised, and rewrote potential letters to be sent to the school superintendent. Following is the letter the children decided to send.

> Dear Mr. Owen,
>
> For the past several weeks, we have been researching the many uses of math within the everyday functioning of Canada's Wonderland. It is our hope that in doing so you will be able to see that such a trip would not only be a tremendous amount of fun, but would also be educational. We sent a letter to Mr. Morley in hope that he would approve our trip, but he said that the rules in place would make it very difficult for him to do so. We are hoping that you can help us in our hope of going to Canada's Wonderland for our end-of-the-year school trip. We have enclosed copies of our math investigation journals in which we did all of our research. You will see that we have found many everyday uses of mathematics at Canada's Wonderland.
>
> Sincerely,
>
> Mr. Muise's Grade 5–6 Students

Unfortunately, the children never did hear back from the superintendent. They did, however, inquire further with Mr. Morley, who continued to say that without the school board's approval he would not be able to grant permission to go on a trip to Canada's Wonderland.

For the most part, the parents were completely supportive of the children's wishes for their trip. When Mike asked what convinced them such a trip would be a good thing, many of the parents pointed to the math investigation journals as viable data that demonstrated the children had grown academically. Although they were unable to fulfill their hopes of going to Canada's Wonderland, Mike felt it was one of the most exciting experiences for both him and his students.

Critically Reading and Interrogating School Practices

In spite of the fact that the letter writing and research failed to bring about desired results, Mike was pleased to have had the opportunity for his students to examine the everyday uses of math. In addition, and perhaps more importantly, they had an opportunity and willingness to act on what they believed and to interrogate what they deemed a problematic school practice. Their initiating experience, born out of Malcolm's response to the book *If . . .* , provided an opportunity to critically examine existing school practices.

From Mike's vantage point, discussions that resulted from reading the book provided his students with the what-if metaphor, creating a forum through which his own shortcomings as an educator became visible to him.

> Mike: Before the discussions that followed our reading *If . . .* , I believed that by providing my students with choices I was able to support my quest for democracy within my classroom. What I was failing to see was how my choices were also limiting rather than generative.

Through the discussions and research that culminated in the exchange of letters, Mike's students learned that the decisions about the kind of knowledge that counts in schools are made not only by students and teachers in classrooms but also by individuals outside of the classroom—by the school administrators. Even though the children in his class had worked diligently researching practical everyday uses of mathematics, convincing school administration that such knowledge is viable and valuable, school board officials ultimately make decisions as to the kind of knowledge that should be valued in classrooms.

Regardless, Mike and his students learned a great deal. His students challenged him to examine how he was attempting to create a democratic classroom. He in turn learned where he was failing to do so. As a community, the students discovered that not everything is distributed equally. Most important, they discovered that power is unequally distributed within the school system. Even though Mike was the person they worked with each school day, there are those outside of the classroom, some who may never see the inside of their classroom or get to know them, who are nevertheless the ones who make decisions about what they can and cannot do. They learned that those in positions outside the classroom value particular kinds of knowledge. As such their story is not just about doing math at an amusement park. It is about disrupting dominant school practices about what counts as learning and where that learning best unfolds. In the end, Malcolm had this to say as a result of asking "What if?": "I have learned more from planning this trip than any other, even if we didn't get to go!"

Reflection Questions

1. Make a list of the various ways that you have used writing in your classroom beyond the language arts curriculum and, in particular, in the math curriculum. What are some other ways that you might use writing in your classroom as a way for your students to act on issues that matter to them? How might you incorporate such writing across the curriculum, including the math curriculum? How might you make that writing curriculum critical?
2. Reflect on the kinds of choices you make available in your classroom. How might you negotiate choices that take into account issues that are important to your students across the content areas?
3. Make a list of the last five texts you read to or with your class. For each text, identify what you did. What kind of work did you hope to accomplish? For what area of the curriculum was each text used? What are some ways that you might use books written for children alongside other everyday texts

and events to set up particular discussions and offer different perspectives in the math curriculum?

Try This

Choosing texts that would work in a particular setting is not always easy. Following are a few suggestions to consider when making your choices.

- Begin by listening closely to the children's interests, questions, inquiry, wonderings, and comments, and then search for books that speak to these.
- Choose books that are generative. In other words, choose books that would encourage diverse and varied responses from children.
- Choose books that are aesthetically interesting in their design, color, form, orientation, and language use.
- Choose books that are accessible and meaningful to your students' experiences and that are culturally relevant to their lives.
- Choose books that reflect mathematical ideas in interesting and creative ways, in diverse settings and places, involving diverse individuals or groups.

Resource Box 4.1 Whitin and Whitin's Problem Posing

A strategy for working with texts developed by Whitin and Whitin (2005) is the problem-posing strategy. This strategy connects nicely with the work Mike and his students have done with the book *If*... Whitin and Whitin explain:

> Problem-posing involves taking a "what-if" stance toward a problem, situation, or story. It consists of describing, modifying and extending the attributes of a story. As children list these attributes, they see a world of related stories embedded within the first story. It has been argued that the more learners change a given story/problem, the better they understand it.

For additional resources and ideas regarding math and children's literature, see the National Education Association's website (http://www.nea.org/home/ToolsAndIdeas.html).

5

Negotiating Critical Literacies Using Science Observations

What's the weather?
What's the weather?
What's the weather?
What's the weather, everyone?
Is it partly cloudy?
Is it cloudy?
Is there rain?
Or is there sun?

What About the Other Weathers?

This song was one that all the first-grade children would sing each morning at the school where Kevan Miller taught. Kevan was part of a study group that I worked with from 2001 to 2007 comprised of teachers from Falls Church, Virginia, USA. Our focus was on finding ways to create spaces for critical literacy in the elementary school classroom. Our commitment to the group included keeping journals or noting opportunities through which to construct critical literacies as well as our attempts at working with children from this perspective. Regarding the opening song, Kevan wrote,

> When trying to create spaces for critical literacy throughout the curriculum, I think it's helpful to notice what your students are noticing. I had been singing the weather song with my first graders since I started teaching and I never really thought much about it one way or the other. I was introduced to the song the year I student taught. My mentor and, as far as I knew, all of the other first-grade teachers sang the song with their first graders as part of the daily calendar routine before math and science time. So when I started teaching at the same school, I sang it, too. Last year was no different, really, except that after the first week of singing the weather song daily, Ronal suddenly looked at me and asked, "Ms. Miller, what about the other weathers?"

While going through the morning routine one day after singing the weather song, Ronal, one of the boys, pointed out that "snowy" wasn't part of the song. At this point the other children began to take notice of what else was missing. "There's no foggy," someone offered. "What about windy?" A conversation then ensued with regards to why only certain kinds of weather are included in the song and who decided what kinds of weather would be included.

Kevan responded, "You're right. What could we do?" In response several children replied, "Make a new song!" In those few moments, Ronal and the other children were beginning to deconstruct the song and reimagine a new version for themselves that included their understanding of the weather. With this, a class science and math project was born.

In this chapter, I spend time in the classroom of Kevan Miller and her first graders as she attempts to frame this newly developed math and science project from a critical literacy perspective. While reflecting on the progress of this project, Kevan noted,

> I'd like to say that it was that easy, that after some brief discussion and planning the children started working on a new song that very afternoon. But I had other things planned, and although I don't remember what they were now, I must have thought they were important at the time. Whatever I had planned for the next day must have been important as well. And the day after that. And the day after that. . . . I loved that Ronal questioned what was

left out of the song, and I loved the idea of the children working together to write a new weather song, but in fact almost three weeks passed before I brought up the topic again. The children brought it up a few times at first. Ronal would point out, again, that "snowy" was left out of the song, and several children would ask, "What about our new weather song?" But there were so many other things to do during the math–science block, and as a half-time classroom teacher I was with this class for such a short time already. The weather song was a small part of our few hours together, and there were so many things they needed to learn. When was there time to write a new song?

Building From Students' Observations

Kevan was certain there wasn't time, but she couldn't stop thinking about Ronal's observation. She knew she was missing an opportunity to build curriculum from an issue that the children clearly wanted to explore. She also knew that if this were going to happen, she would have to make the time and create as much space for this work as she could. She began to feel the pressure of being more and more limited by the school-imposed structure of the day and the short time period assigned to the math and science block. Nevertheless, she decided to push through her anxiety and not worry about the structure and to raise the question regarding the weather song once again. When she finally mentioned the song to the children one afternoon, weeks after they had discussed it, she was met with some blank looks. Kevan worried that she had missed an opportunity to pursue Ronal's insightful question in what could have been a very interesting and transformative project. However, the blank stares quickly disappeared as the children's excitement over the thought of writing a new song returned.

Part of the children's hesitation could have stemmed from Kevan's having put off the discussion in the past so the question of whether this really would happen this time might have been on their minds. She realized that she had positioned their inquiry question regarding the weather as less important than other aspects of the curriculum and now they were unsure as to her intentions.

What was most frustrating for Kevan was not being able to carry out her belief that children learn best when they participate in learning activities and projects that are interesting to them and that have importance in their lives (Comber, 2005; Edelsky, 2000;

Vasquez, 2005a). In her journal, Kevan wrote, "I realized that this was something that was meaningful and important to them. They saw something that needed to be changed, and they wanted to follow through." Johnston (2004) notes, "Starting with the child's observations rather than the teacher's has many advantages. When children notice things instruction can begin with a joint focus of attention because the children are already attending" (p. 18). This was clearly the case in Kevan's classroom.

As the children carried on with their project they shared what they knew about weather. They started with a brainstorming session and listed the types of weather they felt should be included in the song (see Figure 5.1). After much discussion they returned to their

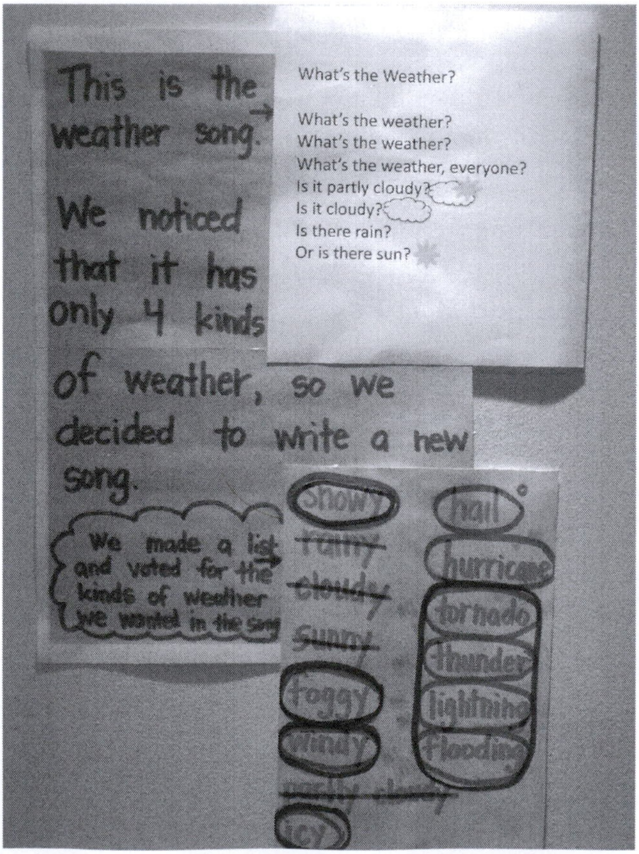

FIG. 5.1 Brainstorming Chart About the Weather

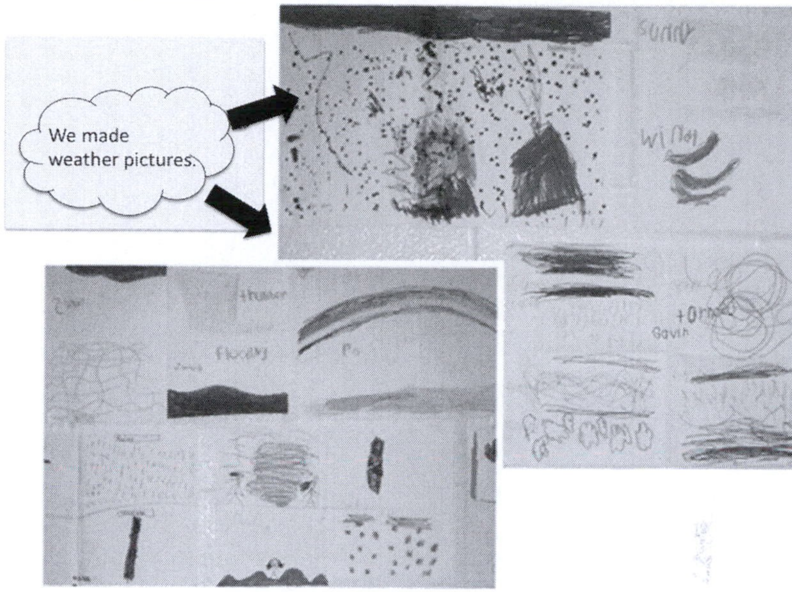

FIG. 5.2 Drawings of the Weather

list and circled the ones they felt were most appropriate based on their experiences. Some of the children also drew images of different kinds of weather (see Figure 5.2). They also searched through various books and resources in the classroom library for weather-related books, sorting them and labeling baskets to hold the different categories of weather they had imagined. They read both fiction and nonfiction books—fiction to get a sense of how weather was represented in various texts and nonfiction to gather information on different kinds of weather and their effects. Finally, they talked about how they might go about rewriting the song.

Tajik: We should keep this song because it has some of the weather.

Gilton: Yeah, we could just add a piece to the bottom.

After more discussion and agreement, the students decided to use the original song as a foundation for adding on their new ideas. In doing so, they added two new verses. What was interesting about their revised song is the way in which they categorized the types

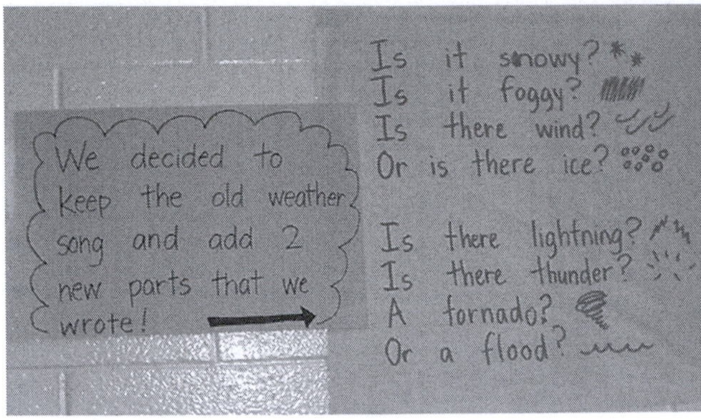

FIG. 5.3 Revised Weather Song

of weather so that one verse dealt primarily with winter weather while the other verse dealt primarily with weather in the spring (see Figure 5.3). Also interesting to note is that during the students' discussion they decided to include "tornado" because some of them had experiences with tornado warnings and talked about these in their homes, even though none of them had actually experienced being in a tornado. They also decided to add flooding and thunder and lightning storms because some of them had experienced such weather. When given a chance to bring to the fore their funds of knowledge (Moll, 1992), children are better able to connect more readily with the curriculum. "Funds of knowledge" refers to the accumulated and culturally based knowledge and skills that are part of the children's experiences, which they bring to the classroom. Finding connections between their lives and the curriculum is what keeps children interested in the work they have before them, often even if that work is complicated or challenging.

The Project Continues

What Kevan didn't realize was that re-writing the weather song was only the beginning of a more involved project. During the time she and her students were working on the song, the children noticed that their weather graph and weather cards, which had been provided in the science kit that all first-grade teachers in the district received, included only certain types of weather as well: sunny, cloudy, rainy, and snowy.

Gilton: Who made the weather graph and cards?
Teacher: They were sent from the County. All first grades use the same things.
Gilton: Do all the first grades sing a song, too?

Kevan reflected,

> With Gilton's remark, our world became a little bit bigger. This wasn't just about our first-grade class anymore. The children realized that the song, the graph, and the weather cards that we used every day were created by someone else, information was missing, and other first grades were (similarly) affected.

Gilton's question moved what had been a very local classroom-based event into a broader arena: the school as a whole and the school district. Part of the discussion dealt with why all first graders have to sing the same song and who made the decision for this to happen. Being unable to respond to the question brought home the notion of the randomness of some decision making carried out in the creation and distribution of school curriculum. In Kevan's reflection, she considers how the use of specific mandated materials position her students in particular ways. There are assumptions being made regarding what children in first grade should know in the science curriculum, about weather (four kinds of weather), what children are capable of knowing (a limited understanding of weather), and how they should come to this knowing (through the use of the song and chart). She was, therefore, excited to see how the original song-writing project generated other activities and learning. Having rewritten the song, the children began talking about with whom they ought to share.

Abha: Let's share our song with first grade.
Tajik: No, maybe everybody. Kindergarten, 2nd, 3rd, 4th . . .
Gilton: Yes, everybody!
Tajik: How can we do that?
Abha: The news!

The children had seen other classes sharing artwork, writing, and skits on the school's daily news program, which was shown on the TV monitors in each of the classrooms. Therefore this was an obvious venue for them and a venue that they felt would give their song some exposure. After some conversation regarding what they should do for the in-school telecast, Kevan and her students videotaped a segment that included Abha, Tajik, and Gilton describing the original, limited version of the weather song followed by a class performance of the redesigned version of the song. Their segment aired on the news later that week.

Redesigning the Weather Graph

Feeling a sense of accomplishment with having rewritten the song and having performed the song as a demonstration to the rest of the school that things do not have to be as they are, the children moved on to redesign the weather graph. What is interesting about the weather graph is that although it accompanies the song in the weather "kit," the types of weather presented in each is not consistent. The children called attention to this detail as well and kept this in mind as they created their version of the weather graph. Their initial work at trying out the newly revised graph is shown in Figure 5.4. Here the children basically took a copy of the existing graph and created additional columns and rows to try it out and see how it might look.

FIG. 5.4 Trying Out the Re-Designed Weather Graph

Abha created the new chart and included symbols to represent each type of weather listed. Creating the new chart, including deciding how big to make the columns and rows, provided more opportunities for doing science and math than just filling in squares for a bar graph. The final version of the newly created chart is shown in Figure 5.5.

The children also began writing surveys to try to find out what other first graders knew about weather: "What kind of weather do you like?" and "What is your favorite weather?" They also surveyed other classes to find out if they might want a new weather graph (see Figure 5.6).

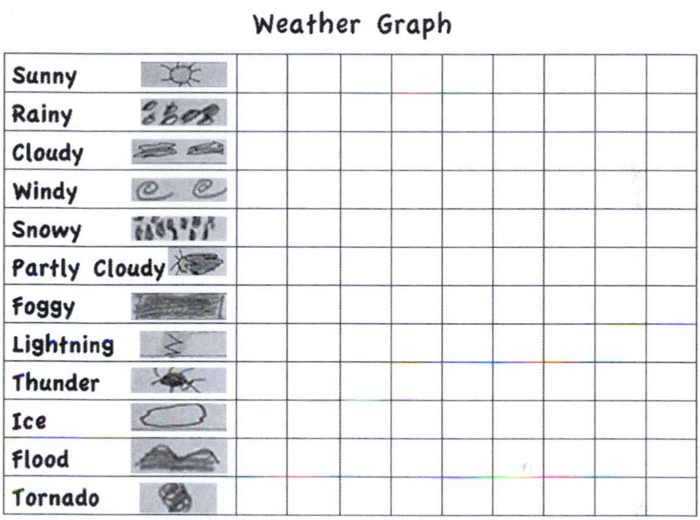

FIG. 5.5 The Final Re-Designed Weather Graph

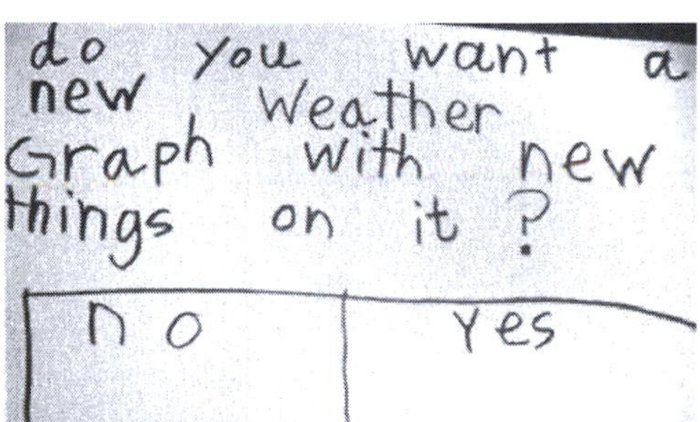

FIG. 5.6 Survey Given to Other Classes

One afternoon the children worked in pairs and surveyed every first-grade class. They presented their revised weather graph and tallied how many students were interested in having a copy of the graph for their class and how many were not. A few of the children encountered some resistance to the new graph. One boy challenged Gilton and Jose: "But we can't have tornadoes here, or floods." When Gilton and Jose shared this with the class, Kevan asked them what they thought about the comment:

Gilton: No! We disagree.
Jose: He can think that. It's OK.

By saying "It's OK," Jose acknowledges that people can have different points of view in spite of Gilton's use of the collective "we" to strengthen his disagreement with the boy. Part of understanding that texts are socially constructed is knowing that different perspectives are represented in their construction and that there is nothing natural or neutral about any of those perspectives. As text readers, whether we agree or disagree matters less than being as informed a reader as possible. This includes understanding that even our own readings of those texts are not neutral and that, as we read, we do so using our past experiences and our beliefs or ideologies. The feedback the children received also helped them to understand the effects of the text, they had created, on others.

The responses the children received were generally positive, and some classes were curious about making their own weather graph. When it came time to distribute the revised graph to the other first grades, the children decided to include the steps they took to redesign the graph. This was a nice way for them to make visible how they came to re-design it as they did. Said differently, the position from which they engaged in the re-design (their beliefs and process) was made transparent for others.

In the end, through the weather project the children did not just accomplish the skills required of them from the Virginia Standards of Learning (Virginia Department of Education, n.d.), they surpassed what was required of them. Table 5.1 demonstrates this notion. On the left side of the chart are two of the standards, one each for science and math. On the right side of the chart are the various skills experienced and learned by the children by participating in the weather project.

TABLE 5.1
The Paper Curriculum Versus the Lived Curriculum

Virginia Standards of Learning	What happened in Kevan's Classroom
Science: The student will investigate and understand basic types, change, and patterns of weather. Key concepts include temperature, wind, precipitation, drought, flood, and storms. Math: Probability and Statistics The student will read, construct, and interpret a simple picture and bar graph.	Science and Math: • Explored, researched, and discussed different types of weather and where they occurred. • Key concepts included a discussion on wind, fog, flooding, snow storms, rainstorms, tornadoes, and hurricanes. • Surveyed types of weather to be included. • Read, analyzed, constructed, and designed a weather chart in the form of a bar graph. • Created and presented new weather song. • Used technology in creating a video for the school news.

Remaining Open to Ideas and Alternatives

Creating space for the children to interrogate, de-construct, and rewrite the weather song, as well as redesign the weather graph, made visible the notion that texts are socially constructed and, therefore, texts can be recreated or redesigned. This notion is one of the key tenets of critical literacy. This in and of itself, however, does not constitute critical literacy. However, it does create space for doing critical literacy work, such as advocating for change and understanding the points of view from which texts are created. For instance, as the children problematized the weather song and chart, they did so from the point of view of children who have experienced different kinds of weather. Having experienced different kinds of weather—including flooding, for instance—helped them to read the weather song and chart as problematic because these did not represent their experiences.

In a final reflection on this project, Kevan wrote,

> There will always be other things to do, plans and obligations that compete for our attention. But what *we* attend to the *children* will attend to, so we need to be open to other ideas and alternatives. We must listen to and acknowledge the conversations in our classrooms, and make time for the opportunities that are presented to us.

Reflection Questions

1. In this chapter, Kevan Miller, the classroom teacher, argues that in order to best support our students, we need to find ways to "notice what they are noticing." What are some things you might do to notice what children are noticing? How might you record those noticings? What might you do to build curriculum using these?
2. Reflect on a time when you might have put the children's ideas, questions, wonderings aside in order to 'cover' the mandated curriculum. Think about what you might have done differently? What kinds of support might you have needed? How might you go about getting the support that you need?

Try This

- Listen closely to the issues your students raise during discussion time or during small-group conversation. Make a list of these issues. How might you explore issues from a critical science perspective?
- Think about one of the issues you noticed your students raising. What resources might you use to further explore this issue? What books and multimedia texts might be useful?
- Jot down some ideas regarding how you might use the issues raised by children to negotiate a science-focused critical literacy curriculum.

6

Critical Literacy and the Social Studies Curriculum

Eduardo: If they are trying to save trees, then why would they give us pencils?
Siena: What?
Eduardo: Pencils. Duh!

Re-Thinking Arbor Day

On January 4, 1872, J. Sterling Morton proposed a tree-planting holiday that has come to be known as Arbor Day. Ten years later, in 1882, Arbor Day became a nationwide celebration, which eventually became a ritual celebrated in schools across the United States. Such was the case in spring 2005 when Eduardo and Siena, two of Sarah Vander Zanden's fifth-grade students, were chosen to represent their class at a tree-planting ceremony sponsored by the student council of their school. A few students from each class were invited to a special dedication service, as student representatives, to plant a tree to commemorate Arbor Day. The opening conversation took place as Eduardo and Siena returned to their classroom. The pencils they refer to were those distributed to each participant at the end of the ceremony, as a symbol to remember the day and what it meant. After overhearing the conversation, in her journal, Sarah wrote,

> I keep thinking about what Eduardo had said. His question was a generative question; it would propel the discussion forward. I knew this because the kids were learning about conservation, and we had read books about this. I expected that they would be able to grasp Eduardo's observations about the contradiction in handing out a wooden pencil to celebrate trees. It was the contradiction, the thought process and observation that mattered.

Sarah had been part of a critical literacy study group. This is in fact the same study group to which Carol Felderman, whom you will meet in chapter 11; Kevan Miller, whom you met in chapter 5; and Christine Paul, who you will meet in chapter 12, belonged. Sarah, along with others in the study group, kept a journal of literacy moments and events that unfolded in their classrooms. Sharing these moments and events was an important aspect of participating in the group.

Reflective writing was a tool Sarah used to rethink her teaching practice as one way of better supporting her students' needs. In her journal she wrote about and reflected on larger issues her students were raising. She also wrote about intersections between the real curriculum in her classroom and the mandated curriculum of the state of Virginia. The pencil incident is a good example of this point of intersection, whereby the mandated social studies curriculum that resulted in the Arbor Day celebration resulted in the underlying issue of conservation raised by Eduardo when he asked, "If they are trying to save trees, then why would they give us pencils?"

This point of intersection is further illuminated in the following journal entry.

> Sarah: Eduardo had noticed a contradiction and was raising questions about this observation in a respectful way. He was a "special" participant, one of a select few who could attend this dedication. We had read a lot about conservation in the weeks building up to this event and discussed them as a class. We had studied erosion, weathering, and human impact on the Chesapeake watershed through fieldtrips, in class experiments, and research in the first quarter

> of the school year. I included some texts that would reinforce key curricular ideas surrounding landforms and human impact on the land, as specified in the Fairfax County POS (Program of Study) and Virginia Standards of Learning (SOLs), because it was now the third quarter and the year-end high stakes tests were coming.

Even though Sarah fully believed in, and was very good at, building social studies curriculum from the interests of her students, she was very cognizant of what children were expected to know to be successful at the high-stakes tests that they would have to take. Knowing the demands of the mandated curriculum made it easier for Sarah to engage in teaching practices she felt would be most supportive of her students' inquiry questions and interests because she was able to identify where the mandated content was addressed in this non-mandated work.

Setting a Context for Social Issues in the Social Studies Classroom

During one of our study group meetings, Sarah shared her experiences in working with her students to focus on class discussion as a means to articulate their opinions and advocate for their needs and as a way of promoting access to the school curriculum for her fifth-grade students who might struggle in academic settings. The class was her first "official" experience with an inclusion classroom. She had always had seven or so students with learning differences in her class, but she had never had as many English-language learners at varying levels of second language acquisition, and more than 60% of the class on free or reduced-cost lunch because their family's income fell below the poverty line. This year's class was definitely one of the most linguistically and culturally diverse groups of children with whom she had ever worked.

In a journal entry she shared with the group, she wrote,

> Although all of the classes at the school had many speakers of other languages, the range of languages and experiences in this group was the most diverse I had worked with yet. Students and their families' came from 12 countries (Pakistan, Guatemala, Mexico, El Salvador, Cuba, Nicaragua, Costa Rica, Philippines,

> Cambodia, Laos, Nigeria, and the United States) and spoke at least 12 different languages before English. Two of the 21 were English speakers first. Most students spoke at least two languages, their home language and English, with varying ranges of English proficiency. Three of the students were bilingual in Spanish and English and participated in the Spanish Immersion class. Another way the class was diverse aside from linguistic diversity was that this class was also a designated inclusion class. This meant many students with specific learning needs (half of the group) were intentionally placed in our co-taught classroom. One student had full-time assistance due to significant physical needs, while others students benefited from extra support during the co-taught language arts block. Though many students had academic needs, there were also many who excelled academically, for example five students were involved in the county gifted and talented program.
>
> Students' life experiences also varied greatly. When I asked the class to share stories of how they came to the school as a way to get to know each other, stories including tracing how their families came to the United States. This year stories included describing the Killing Fields in Cambodia, political persecution in Nicaragua and El Salvador, tracing the history of a former slave family from South Carolina, a father pursuing a graduate degree in the U.S., as well as moving from another part of the county or from another state. Many shared their families' general hopes for a better education for their children. Not all of the stories students shared were extreme, but they were different and illustrated for me the unique makeup of the class.

While keeping her students in mind, in another journal entry Sarah wrote,

> My goal [this year] was for all of the students to be active participants in class, so we spent a great deal of time cultivating a classroom community devoted to listening to one another and learning how to accept that different kids have different needs and that was OK. I explicitly taught kids how to disagree in the classroom and on the playground, as well as how to notice what others were doing so that we could be more respectful of our classmates and be better peer supports in academic settings.

Sarah and her students also engaged in many civics-oriented projects, such as collecting materials needed by an animal shelter and exploring environmental conservation. As part of this work, Sarah read literature and various other resources that helped her students think differently about certain topics or issues or that provided different ways of thinking about an issue or topic. She believed offering her students ways of looking at things from multiple perspectives was an important life skill. She often used books, both fiction and nonfiction, to provide such perspectives and as a jumping off point for discussion. As a group, Sarah and her students read books like *Stand Tall, Molly Lou Melon* (Lovell & Catrow, 2002), which deals with issues of difference; *Seed Folks* (Fleischman, 2004), which focuses on participation in community; and *The Wump World* (Peet, 1991), where aliens use up Earth's resources. This last book, in particular, sparked lots of discussion about the impact our everyday actions have on the world around us, and heightened the group's awareness of observing the world from an environmentalist perspective. Consequently, Sarah's students were not naïve when it came to taking on projects focused on social issues. This is the background experience that framed Eduardo's question regarding the Arbor Day pencil. It is a good reminder of what difference it makes to put on offer more powerful discursive practices in the classroom because, after all, our students can only ever speak using the discourses for which they have access or that they have experienced. In critiquing the Arbor Day event, Eduardo puts into play perspectives that have come through the work Sarah and her students had done in their classroom.

Plant a Tree and Make the World a Better Place

In one of her journal entries, Sarah talks about the generativeness of Eduardo's question, especially given the experience the children had previously with issues regarding the environment and conservation. She notes that Eduardo making problematic the contradiction in handing out pencils at an Arbor Day celebration is what would make the difference. She was right. His question resulted in sustained conversation about the issue.

Sarah wondered what her other students thought about the Arbor Day incident and hoped that Eduardo's comment would generate topics for study. Conversation during class meeting had been a successful venue for the majority of her students to participate throughout the year and she wanted to take the opportunity to explore how much some of the children had grown in this respect. The comment came from Eduardo, a student who had been less engaged in the class since the beginning of the year. Despite how hard Sarah tried to keep the curriculum accessible to him, there were many times when he found it difficult to participate and seemed disinterested in the topics being studied. Nevertheless, Sarah continued to work with him on repositioning himself in the classroom, by doing things like identifying people with whom he might want to work or creating space for him to join in classroom conversations by helping him articulate his ideas. She had hoped to make learning more accessible and interesting for him. She tried to help him find classmates with whom he shared common interests and tried to draw out of him what topics and issues he was interested in pursuing.

Sarah brought the children together for discussion. While the group sat around a circle, she started the conversation by restating what Eduardo had said the day before. Her students were used to discussion and had often sat in the circle for class meeting, book discussions, and content lessons. Early on in the year she had spent time with them on what it means to have respectful conversations. She talked with her students about the importance of turn taking during discussion time. She also talked with them about it being acceptable to disagree with one another as long as during the conversation each student who had something to say was given an opportunity to do so. She shared with them that class meeting time was as an opportunity to talk with others in the class about their burning issues, such as the Arbor Day incident. This process was, therefore, familiar to them.

Teacher: What do you think about what Eduardo said?

Immediately the fifth graders jumped into the conversation:

Ansony: So what if they give you a pencil? I didn't get one.
Sanya: They could have given you a paper to share at home; I would share it.
Milton: Maybe they thought that if they gave papers, kids would throw them and they won't throw pencils.

Ansony's comment and the responses by Sanya and Milton are representative of the effects of the normalized or naturalized treatment of Arbor Day in many school settings where students participate in set rituals as passive observers. It is easy to see how this normalization comes into being when looking more closely at resources available to teachers regarding celebrating this day. For instance, phrases like "Celebrate Arbor Day and take positive action" or "Celebrate Arbor Day to make the world a better place" represent the sorts of sentiments that pepper resource documents on Arbor Day. In an Internet search on "Studying Arbor Day" or "Unit of Study on Arbor Day," for instance, I found resources like the Arbor Day Alphabetic Order Worksheet from www.teachnology.com and a cloze activity called Clozing the Deal on Arbor Day from www.teachers.net, whereby students are asked to identify 12 words having to do with Arbor Day, learn to recite and use these words, and then use the words in context by means of a class sentence bee.

Neglected are opportunities to historicize and unpack the day as one with political roots whereby people who moved into the Nebraska Territory in the 1800s proposed the holiday at a meeting of the State Board of Agriculture and where eventually what has come to be known as Arbor Day came into being as a result of an official proclamation. Lost are opportunities to explore reasons beyond "greening" as the impetus for such a day. For instance, Heger (2000) notes that J. Sterling Morton, who founded Arbor Day in 1872, was an ardent opponent of the tariff protecting the US lumber industry from foreign competition and that he had another motive behind his Arbor Day advocacy. According to Heger (2000),

> [Morton] detested the protective tariff that enriched the U.S. lumber industry and depleted native forests. He wanted to break the power of the tariff. So his secondary Arbor Day message was: Plant a tree and strike a blow for free trade.
>
> (p. 3)

This is a far cry from the passive save-the-world-through-celebration rhetoric in "Celebrate Arbor Day and make the world a better place."

Re-Designing Existing Practice: Make the World a Better Place

As the conversation continued, the students began to come up with alternate solutions, in a "redesign" of what artifact, other than a pencil, could have been handed out at the event. This sustained conversation, of which a portion is included below, resulted from the children's desire to get the message out regarding ways of respecting the environment, to more than just the special group who was allowed to attend the Arbor Day event.

Eduardo: We need to save trees, save the environment, not cut down trees. They are lying.
Teacher: Who is "they"?
Reston: Professionals who protect trees. Probably.
Siena: The PTA.
Teacher: Why?
Siena: They got the tree.
Eduardo: The government.

As the children continued to unpack the context in which the event took place, they began a conversation about the larger systems in place and how things are decided. Gee (2004) refers to these social ways of being as systems of meaning. He describes these systems as comprised of complex interactions and relationships that shape the way things are. These are held in place by discourses, a community's ways of doing, being, thinking, acting, and so forth. The children recognize that things don't just happen; there are decision makers out there and there is nothing natural or neutral about the process of deciding the way the day is celebrated and what memento might be appropriate to represent the day. This lends itself to the development of a worldview that is more active than reactive. If you can identify the decision makers—those in power and the interests they serve—you can then think in a different way about the decisions being made, generate new ideas, and contribute to disrupting the problematic practice and contribute to change.

Mei-an: Yeah, maybe they have so much extra wood that they made pencils for the kids.
Siena: Yeah, it could be recycled wood. (Examines pencil)
Eddy: Well, where do they [pencils] come from? Why not use plastic instead of wood?
Claro: Well, when they cut down the trees, they have to plant another one. So maybe they did that. But they could just make a commercial and not cut down any trees and everyone would see it, not just Cheto and Siena. I mean, fliers and pencils both use wood and we don't even know what they wanted now . . . because we weren't there.

As the group considers alternate perspectives, Claro noticed his classmates struggling with the issue of "the Arbor Day pencil." In response, he begins directly teaching about tree conservation when he says, "Well, when they cut down trees, they have to plant another one . . ." He also talks about how to make this kind of information accessible to a wider audience stating, "they could just make a commercial . . . and everyone would see it. . . ." He also raises the issue of not knowing the position from which the Arbor Day event was planned, saying, "we don't even know what they wanted . . . because we weren't there." In other words, Claro makes the point that they do not really know the intent of the event planners in handing out the pencil or why they chose such an artifact to commemorate the day. He knows there is an underlying message that comes with the event but what that is exactly is unclear. Nevertheless, acknowledging that someone wanted to get some message across demonstrates Claro's knowledge that texts, including the event as a "text" to be read, are socially constructed and that they are constructed from particular perspectives, beliefs, and ideologies. This goes along with Sarah's belief of the notion that the world, events, places, things, print matter, and so forth, can all be read, interpreted, and analyzed in some way.

The conversation continued.

Christian:	I disagree; factories have to make pencils, and they use energy so they might cut down more and just use the extra wood to do the pencils.
Reston:	I disagree with Eddy, because we can't sharpen plastic pencils. Mechanical would be better.
Marisol:	You can sharpen plastic pencils.
Michael:	Yeah, lead is better, mechanical.
Reston:	Wait, I disagree with Michael now, even though they wouldn't use wood, they are using other resources. Which resource is better? It's like *The Wump World* [Peet, 1991]. Wait—how do you get lead?

In this exchange, the students begin to stray from the underlying social issue as they discuss whether plastic or mechanical pencils would be better. Eventually they return to *The Wump World*, highlighting the human impact on the environment and making connections to information previously learned through class work about resources and energy. Since the beginning of the school year, the children had gotten better at using one text (e.g., *The Wump World*) to read another text (Arbor Day as a social text). They have learned that to better critically analyze a situation, one needs to frame it using a different discursive perspective. *The Wump World* created a space for them to do this. Framing their understanding of the Arbor Day event from the lens of *The Wump World* helped the children to better articulate their thinking.

Kazin: For real, if they gave mechanical pencils they would waste more money for them. It's just a dumb reminder; they wouldn't waste that much money on us.

Kazin's comments were made out of frustration over the distribution of the pencil and the conversations with his classmates. He had felt that some of his classmates should have been more concerned about the underlying issues or conservation. His comments during the class meetings on this topic focused on different possible realities. Were pencils distributed as an inexpensive and unnecessary token? Was this inexpensive token reflective of the organizers attitude, specifically that "pencils were good enough for the children"? When Kazin says, "they wouldn't waste that much money on us," he is referring to any memento that might cost more than a pencil, such as a mechanical pencil. Either way he felt that little thought was given to the event as a whole, thus his reference to the pencils as "dumb reminders."

The idea of reminders is an interesting one when set in the context of schools as rule governing institutions. Was the pencil meant to be a reminder of the moral lessons associated with the event, whatever those may have been? If so, Kazin seemed almost insulted that such a reminder was felt by the organizers to be necessary.

Gabriela: Who decided it anyways? Maybe we should write a letter.

To get responses to some unanswered questions regarding the decision-making process around Arbor Day, and as a form of social action, Gabriela suggests writing a letter. She made this recommendation based on her past experiences and success in getting issues resolved through letter writing. For instance, in the past she had written a letter to be included in the yearly special education conference her parents attended at her school regarding how to best support her learning. Eduardo, Siena, and Kazin, who first noticed the ridiculousness of distributing pencils on Arbor Day, took up Gabriela's suggestion and wrote a letter to the Parent–Teacher Association. Further, they submitted comments on a couple of websites focused on Arbor Day. Siena also met with the student council association president and staff representative about making the Arbor Day ceremony accessible to all students instead of limiting the event to a chosen few.

The Arbor Day incident took place at the end of the school year when the fifth graders were about to leave the school to attend a middle school nearby. Sarah, the classroom teacher, also left the school to pursue doctoral studies. Unfortunately, as a result, there was no follow up on what resulted from the letter writing and meeting with the student council president and staff representative. After the fact, Sarah did hear that the staff representative, who eventually took on the role of assistant principal at another school, disagreed with the students' concerns and found nothing problematic about privileging some students by inviting them to attend the Arbor Day event while marginalizing others when they are flatly denied an opportunity to do so.

Critical Literacy as Changing Participation

Barton and Hamilton (1998) note,

> Literacy is primarily something people do; it is an activity, located in the space between thought and text. Literacy does not reside in people's heads as a set of skills to be learned, and it does not just reside on paper captured as texts to be analyzed. Like all human activity, literacy is essentially social, and it is located in the interaction between people.
>
> (p. 3)

The interactions engaged in by Sarah's students provided for them space to imagine how existing social practices could be otherwise. This work not only addresses the school district's standards of learning (5.7f), but surpasses the identified key concept: human impact (on the environment). Within the context of attempting to disrupt problematic Arbor Day practices at their school, they began to consider how what they had come to know and believe is shaped by "specific participants in a literacy event and the context itself" (Larson & Marsh, 2005, p. 11). In their letter writing and subsequent meetings with the student council representatives, they began to interrogate the decisions made by these participants as well as the notions associated with the normalized Arbor Day celebration. At the same time, they were gaining experience in reimagining a problematic school practice, which helped them to consider ways they could participate differently in the world of school and beyond. As suggested by Janks and Comber (2005), involving young people in the process of text production, editing, and design demonstrates to them that texts are not neutral or natural. This work also helps young people to understand that language is a powerful tool for doing different sorts of life work and that how we constitute things and how we are constituted through social practice makes a difference in the ways we are positioned in life and the positions from which we are able to speak or participate in the world.

Larson and Marsh (2005) note that people learn by participating in culturally valid activities. Even though the letter writing and the meetings may not have been successful in accomplishing the work the children had imagined, the experience provided a space for them to participate differently in school as active players rather than passive recipients of school and everyday texts.

Reflection Questions

1. Think about the various events held at your setting along with traditions that have been passed on over the years at your institution. Reflect on how these events and traditions were started, by whom, and for what purposes. Whose interests are served by holding such events? Are there those for whom such events are not accessible?
2. In light of the Arbor Day pencil incident, reflect on the language used to describe such events as well as the symbols used to represent these events.

Try This

How might you use social texts such as school events and traditions from which to build a critical social studies curriculum?

To get started, make a list of all school events and celebrations. You could do this in preparation for when it might come up in conversation with your students and as a 'planning to plan' type resource for later use. You could also do this with your students.

For each of the events or celebrations, ask:

- What is the intent of the event or celebration? How do you know?
- Who participates in planning the event?
- Who participates in the actual event? Who is left out?
- Who decides who gets to participate?
- Whose interests are served by the event?
- Whose interests are trivialized or marginalized by the event?
- What could be done to re-think or re-design the event?
- What difference would the re-designed event make, for whom, and in what way?
- Does the event support multilingual learners?

7

Acting Out

Using Process Drama to Read Critically

Lauren:	They're just watching!
Teacher:	Why are they just watching?
Chase:	Because they don't care what happens to black people.
Teacher:	What do you think? If you saw this out in the street, what would you want to do?
Ethan:	I'd kick their butt.
Melissa:	I'd call the police.
Tommy:	I'd beat them up and run.
Teacher:	You have to think of your own safety too, right?
Melissa:	They might have guns.
Ethan:	But what if they do have guns, you never know.
Chase:	Trip them and knock them out. Then say, "Who got the gun now?"
Teacher:	I'm asking you what you are able to do. You might want to go over there and beat them up, but you can't do that because you will probably get hurt.

Lauren: But when someone's fighting like that you should go over there and help them.
Teacher: How can you help? What can you do?
Sean: Call the police!
Tommy: You can talk them out of it.
Emily: OK, pretend I have a gun and I'm about to shoot you. What are you going to do? Talk me out of it. Talk me out of it. (She uses her hand to mimic a handgun, points and waves it at Tommy and begins speaking loudly.) I'm crazy. I'm drunk. Talk me out of it. I'm the one with the gun. Talk me out of it.

This exchange marked a critical moment in Susan Adamson's work with a group of third graders as they focused on making sense of the world through deconstructing and analyzing picture books in light of their own experiences. Up until this moment, Susan struggled with what to do with topics related to issues of power and control in the classroom. However, what happened at the end of the exchange, when the children spontaneously used drama as a tool for meaning making and making sense of a challenging social issue, gave her pause. Their animated voices and bodies drove home the importance of creating spaces and opportunities for children to take up such challenging issues in the classroom. Susan noted,

> The children struggled with their sense of individual power and significance in relationship to their world. Their outrage was potent, a palpable strength of their knowing, but they were rendered impotent as no reasonable course of action occurred to them. Undaunted they continued to explore a repertoire of actions using their own personal text to guide them.

Taking Up Issues of Power and Control in the Classroom

The conversation at the start of this chapter stemmed from a read aloud of the picture book *White Wash* (Shange, 1997), which was the same book that Lee Heffernan and her students worked with in chapter 2. In this chapter an underlying question is what ways can process drama, in combination with other texts, contribute to creating space for children to work through struggles regarding issues of power in their local settings? What kinds of strategies might classroom teachers put in place to help them make sense of that world? How might children use the texts of their everyday lives to read children's books and what role might drama play in these readings? These are a few of the questions asked by Susan while she worked with a group of seven third graders in an urban public school in a midwestern US town. Her reflection deals with her students' responses to the book and the difficulty they experienced when making sense of the racism presented in the text. Observing their emotional reaction to the text and seeing the children animate their bodies in response by moving around the space they occupied and motioning with their arms and hands, Susan decided to use process drama to take up issues of power and control in the book. The result was engaging in social action at their school site to specifically address racism and violence on the playground.

In her reflection, Susan commented on how the children undauntedly continued to explore their repertoire of possible actions. The children's repertoire of actions included using process drama as a way of constructing meaning and unpacking text. In this case, they unpack *White Wash* (Shange, 1997) using what they already knew about "acting out" scenarios to make sense of new experiences. What is most interesting about Susan's work, as described in this chapter, is her venture into process drama as a tool to help her students use the book *White Wash* to take up issues of violence and racism. O'Neill and Lambert (1983) note that process drama as a mode of learning creates spaces for learners of any age to imagine roles and to use these roles to "explore issues, events, and relationships" (p. 11).

The opening discussion took place after Susan read *White Wash* to her group. Susan noted how the children overtly struggled with their sense of individual power and significance during the conversation. The conversation continued:

Ethan: Scream bloody murder.
Melissa: Say "fire." "Fire!" That's what my Mom says to do.
Chase: That's what my Mom says, too. Even if they have a gun and tells you not to scream. You scream.
Emily: What if they have a knife?
Teacher: That's a really big dilemma because you have to decide whether to scream, and if you do they might harm you.

The children felt an urge to act out this scenario. They had already started to do this when Emily used her hand to mimic a handgun, and asked Tommy to "Talk me out of it." At first their dramatizations seemed futile as they ultimately dissolved into laughter.

> Susan: At this point Emily had assigned parts to the other students. While she played the part of "herself," she assigned two of the other boys to be her younger brothers and asked Tommy to be the "guy with the knife." Rather than situate them on the street as the children were in the story, her scenario had them in her house in one of the upstairs bedrooms. On her cue, the "brothers" began to cower in the corner while she tried to confront Tommy. As he slinked over, though, with his arm extended as if holding a knife, they all dissolved into laughter, falling on the floor or collapsing in a chair. But they quickly regrouped, clamoring to try new parts; "Let me try, let me try," they shouted, as if they were more up to the task than the others were. At each attempt (two or three more), laughter prevailed.

In spite of the laughter, the potential of using process drama to make explicit the children's tensions and anxieties was clear. While reflecting on this experience after the fact, Susan realized that the laughter reflected the children's anxiety with playing roles that had not been part of their schema. Previously they had used drama to act out scenes from books, as they appeared, but not as a way to problem solve to construct new meaning. As the children animated their bodies and their voices as a way to 'read' the text, they seemed surprised at some of their own actions. In their past experiences with drama, every word spoken and every move made was planned and orchestrated in particular ways. This drama that they found themselves in was different—here nothing was pre-planned. Their thoughts and actions emerged through the process as voices and bodies interacted and new ideas, questions, and understandings emerged.

Susan noted that adding to the children's discomfort was their own sense of powerlessness in being unable to figure what to do when faced with such danger. What would they do if something like this were to happen in real life? Process drama provided an opportunity to represent the issues they struggled with using an alternate sign system that helped them act out the complexity of the issue at hand. Medina (2006), in her work with immigrant children, theorizes about the ways in which drama affords opportunities for the children to "begin to articulate . . . ways in which they perceive texts and self" (p. 54). For the third graders, dramatizing in the moment positioned them in a space in between the events that unfolded in the text and their lived experiences, creating spaces for them to begin to consider how the issues in the book intersect with their real lives. In their work on dialogized readings, Edmiston and Enciso (2002) talk about drama as an interpretive tool where "students are not expected to explain the story, rather the students are asked to complicate the apparent perspectives of characters and evaluate the consequences of their actions" (p. 870). In so doing students are better able to bring their own experiences to bear on the topic or issue at hand.

Unpacking the Micropolitics of the Playground

Susan wanted her students to be able to think more explicitly about their own feelings in relation to the inequalities with which they have direct experience (Epstein, 1993; Heffernan & Lewison, 2000). Engaging in process drama afforded an opportunity for the children to bring to the fore and discuss complex social issues in *White Wash*. Now, Susan wanted to switch gears and have the children imagine taking on a social issue unfolding in their own place. They decided to examine the micropolitics of the playground in their school. However, what started out as research on problems in the playground between students morphed into observations of interactions between adults and children and the problematic playing out of power differentials between the two groups.

At the school, students relied on teachers to mediate conflicts. However, what they found while engaging in observations in the playground were instances where they noticed the adults on duty were not responsive to the students seeking their help or assistance. This led to a more in-depth study of behavior on the playground where Susan and the third graders produced data in the form of their observations of negative or problematic interactions between adults and students during recess. Upon sharing their observations with one another, they were disturbed by what they learned. Specifically they recorded many instances where adults treated some children unfairly, ineffectively, or were unresponsive to their needs. Acting on their belief that playground supervision needed to be revisited, they initiated a letter-writing campaign informing the principal of what they deemed to be a major problem that could lead to dangerous situations on the playground.

Luke and Freebody (1997) write that students bring to the classroom available cultural, community, and social resources; texts; and discourses. Said differently, all students come to school with cultural and social experiences and particular ways of saying and doing things. These various experiences, or cultural and linguistic resources, connect in multiple ways. What this means is that learning environments need to be responsive to the cultural discourses that students have access to and are active in, by looking closely at the things that are important to them or that they feel have importance in their lives.

> Susan: The books we read and the conversations we had about those books made the cultural texts of the children I worked with easy to access. The books generated rich discussion of issues such as power, ageism, race, and gender. The students were comfortable expressing their ideas verbally; they appeared to speak openly and honestly. As such, our critical conversations offered several possible insights into how they were negotiating issues of social justice.

According to Susan, in the third-grade classroom there was no shortage of opportunities to engage in important conversations about social justice and equity issues that stemmed from her students' lived experiences. This became more and more clear the longer she worked with the children. It was simply a matter of determining which conversations to pursue. Susan notes that as teachers we must keep in mind Epstein's (1993) notion of children as active in the construction of their own realities and subjectivities and, therefore, potentially active in the deconstruction of dominant ideologies. Dominant ideologies refer to prevalent societal beliefs. These ideologies are socially constructed; that is, they are created through social interactions between and among people. As such, they can be deconstructed and reconstructed. However, even though the children's attempts to resolve the playground issue did not end with a positive resolution, the work they did and the processes and literacies afforded by that work provided Susan and her students with invaluable experiences to inform future actions and projects. While reflecting on the experience as a whole, Susan noted the following.

> Susan: There are clearly many complicating factors in the construction of meaningful ideologies, but giving credence to one's own experience would seem crucial to empowerment and lead to the deconstruction of dominant ideologies. This is at least part of what I understand critical literacy intends to do.
>
> The cultural climate of this school has yet to challenge these students to analyze their beliefs in a way that lets them create their own well-considered belief systems. They were articulate and empathetic regarding issues of social justice and equity, and they saw a flawed system in which their counterpart, the adult, did not always support them. So while they seemed predisposed to act, they were not able to do so because there was no "space" for social action and, therefore, no space for the creation of alternative ideologies. But given the opportunity, these children would surely find their voices. And given their voices, we surely must listen.

Reflection Questions

1. Do you use process drama in your classroom as a way of responding to text? What aspects of drama do you think could be beneficial in your setting? In what ways could they be beneficial? How might you use drama to engage in critical literacy?
2. Think back to a time when you felt your students responded strangely to a text you had read to them or a time when they responded in a way you had not anticipated. What did you

do? How did you react? Jot down a few things that you might have done differently if given an opportunity.

3. Despite their attempts to change interactions between adults and children on the playground, Susan's students were not able to come to a resolution. What might you have done differently? What strategies might you have used?

Try This

One way to help create space for conversations that may lead to social action is by making accessible to children multimodal texts (books and other written texts, films, songs, everyday texts) that lend themselves more readily to critical discussions regarding issues of social justice and equity as it plays out in media. Harste, Leland, Lewison, Ociepka, and Vasquez (2000, p. 507) created a set of criteria that is useful for choosing books that may be effective in this regard. Following is an adaptation of those criteria for use with choosing multimodal texts.

- They make difference visible and create space for exploring what difference makes a difference.
- They explore dominant systems of meaning (systems that position people and groups in particular ways) that operate in society and the spaces in which we reside or carry out our lives.
- They create space for taking action on social issues that have importance in the lives of those taking action.
- They help us to unpack the history behind the topic being explored by giving us an opportunity to hear from those who have been traditionally silenced or marginalized.
- They help us question how people and groups have been positioned in particular ways, by whom and to what ends.

To try your hand at creating a multimodal text set begin by listening and observing closely to your students with an ear for emerging topics and issues. Following this, begin building a text set with multimodal pieces. While your students work with the text set, keep a close eye on the literacies afforded by engaging critically with such texts and how such texts play into the children's dramatic representations of the world around them.

Resource Box 7.1 Drama and Performance Pedagogies

Following are resources for use for exploring the use of drama and performance pedagogies in the classroom. Although some of these are focused on work with adolescents and adults, they are nevertheless informative and provide wonderful insight into dramatic performance as a tool for teaching and learning.

Cahnmann-Taylor, M., & Souto-Manning, M. (2010). *Teachers act up! Creating multicultural learning communities through theatre*. New York: Teachers College Press.

Edmiston, B. & Enciso, P. (2002). Reflections and refractions of meaning: Dialogic approaches to classroom drama and reading. In J. Flood, D. Lapp, J. Squire, & J. Jensen (Eds.), *The handbook of research on teaching the English language arts* (pp. 868–880). Mahwah, NJ: Lawrence Erlbaum.

Edmiston, B., Enciso, P., & King, M. L. (1987). Empowering readers and writers through drama: Narrative theater. *Language Arts*, 64 (2), 219–228.

Medina, C. L., Coggin, L., & Weltsek, G. (2014). Foregrounding emergence, embodiment, and critical practices: Performance pedagogies in literacy methods. In J. Brass & A. Webb (Eds.), *Teaching the English language arts methods: Contemporary methods and practices* (pp. 70–82). New York: Routledge.

Medina, C. L., & Perry, M. (2014). Texts, affects, and relations in cultural performance: An embodied analysis of dramatic inquiry. In P. Albers, T. Holbrook, & A. Seely Flint (Eds.), *New methods in literacy research* (pp. 115–132). New York: Routledge.

8

Getting Critical With Music

When I first started writing this chapter I posted a message on Facebook asking for instances of children engaging with music and creating lyrics for songs. Within minutes, I received numerous replies. Some focused on children playing with or approximating songs in ways that intersect with schooling:

> Dylan is 4 and learning to spell words so she takes the lyrics to BINGO and spells words, like *mommy*, *daddy*, her name, her sister's name, *grandma*, *grandpa*, *Anne* (her babysitter), *princess*, *fairy* . . . you know, all that is important to her!
>
> When Peter was about 5 or so, he was singing along with "Born to Be Wild." He had a toy guitar that played the song. He was shouting "Head out on the highway! Looking for subtraction!"
>
> Jim's parents found him in his crib singing the Beatles' "Let it Be"—except he thought it was an alphabet song: Letter B.
>
> I made up a song when I was 9 years old. It was a song about my name and my home address!

Other stories reflected ways that children come to understand language through use, which sometimes results in interesting lexical selections, as in the following examples.

> I had a (4-year-old) student who would sing, "I got the moves like a jaguar" for "moves like Jagger."
>
> My son Aaron loved "It's a Grand Ole Flag"; instead of singing "high flying flag," he sang "high fivin' flag."

Some instances were stories of songs created to elicit particular emotions or to demonstrate a particular feeling.

> One mom shared that her 5-year-old daughter changed the words to "Under the Bamboo Tree" from *Meet Me in Saint Louis*, singing, "I love-a-you but you don't love me" . . . She said her daughter was clearly mad at her for something!
>
> When our twins were born [5-year-old Poppy] came to the hospital and made up this amazing song about how she was going to take care of them and protect them—I was sobbing!!!

Covers of other songs were created to elicit laughter, as in the following instances:

> My daughter was singing "Oh Lord, won't you buy me a Mercedes Benz. My friends all have horses."
>
> Simon made up a song when he was 5. It went, "Cockroach-eating bugs! Cockroach-eating bugs! Everywhere! Everywhere! Spiders and frogs! Spiders and frogs! I will save you! I will save yoooooooouuuuuu!"

There were also instances shared of children clearly following the rhythm of the music and filling in words to fill the beat, as in the following examples.

> For that "Drift Away" song: "give me the beat boys to free my soul," my grandkid sang "give me the pizza, my feet's not sore . . . "
>
> I used to think the Beatles "Paperback Writer" was saying "Take the back, Right turn." I would sing that at the top of my lungs, when I was about 4.

What is important to note about these examples, and the number of stories that people excitedly shared within minutes of my request for such stories, is that music clearly has had a place in all of these children and adults' lives and that they have used songs in different ways to achieve different ends, including having fun. The instances shared are examples of music and songs that were created for different purposes in different contexts. Interestingly, very little has been done in terms of exploring intersections between music and songs specifically and critical literacies with younger children. There are examples of work done with hip-hop and other more contemporary music genres, but this work has generally taken place with adolescent or adult learners. For instance, Morrell and Duncan-Andrade (2002) have written about how they utilized "Hip-hop music and culture to forge a common and critical discourse that was centered upon the lives of the students, yet transcended the racial divide and allowed [them] to tap into students' lives in ways that promoted academic literacy and critical consciousness" (p. 88). Reflecting on their experiences introducing hip-hop and other elements of popular culture into more traditional dominant curricula led them to believe "that there are countless possibilities for urban educators who wish to jump outside the box and tap into the worlds of their students in order to make more powerful connections with traditional academic texts and affirm, in meaningful ways, the everyday lives of those they teach" (Morrell & Duncan-Andrade, 2002, p. 91).

Mitchell (2016) uses music and race as a central theme in history courses he teaches his high school students. He notes, "In the United States, black artists typically have done the lion's share of the innovating, while white artists (and white-owned record labels) have reaped the lion's share of the financial rewards" (Mitchell, 2016, p. 169). Watson (2016), a middle school teacher, argues for the importance of providing students "several entry points to the lessons" (p. 272) He states, "I layer lessons not only with printed words for students who have strong verbal skills, but I also bring in music, movement activities, and visual components to help address the multiple intelligences of all students" (p. 272). Au (2016) pushes the use of music into the content areas, noting that, for instance, "rap music can be applied to almost any humanities and social sciences theme because of its intense political discourse. There are a number of rap groups with political agendas, and you can find songs with content ranging from nonsensical party lyrics to left-wing revolutionary political outlines" (p. 282).

Picking up on Morrell and Duncan-Andrade's notion of tapping into the worlds of children through music, in this chapter I explore possibilities for creating critical literacies while working with music. To do so I turn to a group of younger children to see what I can learn from what they are already doing, in particular with songs and lyrics.

Taylor Swift, Pizza, and Milkshakes

Taylor Swift is well known to young people as a singer who writes songs about her life and the world around her. It is no surprise to find numerous spoofs and covers of her songs. However, what surprised me is the extent and sophistication through which younger children have joined in the mix, re-writing and performing new versions of her songs. Clearly this is an area I have not explored in any depth, so I readily take in new lessons learned.

Bad Blood Take 2

Cause now I want pizza, don't put on any pepperoni.
If you do I'll tell daddy and you'll get in trouble,
  Missy Hey.
Now we got problems, you can go solve them.
By telling the pizza place cheese please just for me.
Did you have to have to do this.
I thought you would order breadsticks.
You know that I love the dipping sauce.
That comes on the side with it.
Did you have to get me,
pepperoni covered breadsticks.
I think you need a seat.
In the naughty chair until breakfast.
Oh it's so sad to see you in the bad chair.
Me oh my . . .

This version of Taylor Swift's "Bad Blood" was written by Daniella and her twin brother Jacob. They were 9 years old when they crafted these lyrics. Along with the song lyrics, their father Mike also sent a video of Daniella performing the song. In the video it is clear that she has embodied the sentiments and attitudes of the song they created.

Clearly, ordering pizza is a familiar experience and therefore one she can sing about readily. It is also clear that she had a lot of fun performing the song. Although I was not familiar with the original song when I first heard it, it did not take much to be able to sing along with Daniella and Jacob's lyrics. Their words flowed smoothly onto Swift's melody.

With lyrics like "So take a look at what you've done. Cause baby now we got bad blood. Now we got problems. Did you have to do this. I was thinking that you could be trusted," Swift's original lyrics focus on the notion of betrayal and her response to that betrayal. Daniella and Jacobs' lyrics maintain the spirit of the original song, except theirs is about being disappointed that someone got their pizza and breadstick order wrong. Daniella sings, "You know that I love the dipping sauce. That comes on the side with it," yet what was ordered was pepperoni-covered breadsticks.

Similar to the twins, Maisie and her friend, both 8 years old, have also had a hand in re-writing a Swift song. This time the song is "Shake it Off," a song about overcoming the negative things that people think of you and do to you. Her mom also sent audio of her performance and, like Daniella, there clearly was enjoyment in her voice. The original lyrics that Maisie and her friend re-wrote are as follows:

> My ex-man brought his new girlfriend
> She's like, "Oh my God," but I'm just gonna shake it
> And to the fella over there with the hella good hair
> Won't you come on over, baby, we can shake, shake, shake

Here is their version of the song:

> My ex-burger brought his new milkshake
> She's like, "Oh my gosh,"
> Cause I'm just gonna shake it
> To the burger over there with the hella good bun
> Won't you come on over, baby, we can milk, milk, shake!

Maisie's play on words in "To the burger over there with the hella good bun" is quite sophisticated, as is her use of personification to turn Swift's ballad into a humorous song.

While picking glue off her fingers after completing an at-home art project, 3-year-old Elle began making up and singing a song influenced by the song "You Are My Sunshine." (Note: Sister is Elle's younger sister, who is 16 months younger. Gaby is her aunt, who had just returned to the west coast after an extended visit.)

Sister
I love you sister
Little sister
I love you sister
I love Gaby
I love Gaby, so much
And I love you so much
And I love you so much
And I lo . . . ve . . . you
Sunshine
Sunshine
Sunny sunshine
Sun sunshine
My only sunshine
Your golden sunshine

Through her song, 3-year-old Elle makes visible to those listening her story of love for her sister and Gaby. She uses what she knows of "You Are My Sunshine," its rhythm, its melody, and its use of words to create her own ballad.

More than anything, what Daniella, Jacob, Maisie, and Elle, along with the other children whose stories are shared at the start of this chapter, have taught me is what an incredible tool music can be for thinking, constructing meaning, and representing understanding across the curriculum. I would be remiss, however, if I did not caution us to make sure that whatever we do does not take away from the children's enjoyment of working with music and song. I also do not want to suggest that we make children write songs. I think creating the space to let children use music and write songs in the ways described here, when it makes sense for the work they are doing, is one thing, especially for children whose learning is enriched by music. Forcing children to use music in this way, however, is quite another. We would be well informed to heed Rowsell's comment that

"Prior to Beethoven, most music was composed for a purpose (e.g., liturgical services, ceremonial accompaniment). What Beethoven did was to demonstrate that music could be more than an extension of something else" (Rowsell, 2013, p. 34). This is what we want for children. For them to be able to use music to "move beyond immediate contexts, situations and thoughts" (Rowsell, 2013, p. 34), and perhaps even to engage in social action projects.

Save Our School: Music as a Form of Resistance

Helping children understand real-life functions of text is an important component of growing as a critically literate person. A good example of this is work done by the Selsted Primary School community in Kent, England. In 2006, the small rural school, located in Kent, was earmarked for closure. The families whose children attended the school were devastated, as many of the children's family members had themselves attended the school. As such it was a place with a rich history in the community. In an attempt to prevent the closure from happening, one of the actions taken by the student and parent community was to write a song and perform it as a form of protest. Lucky for them, music producer Steve Harvey heard of their plight and volunteered to help them write and record the song, which they did. Not only did they write, perform, and record the song, they also created a music video.

The song, titled "Save Our School," included lyrics such as, "Don't close our school. It's been here for many years. My mum and dad both came here too. It's closure will mean tears." The upbeat and catchy chorus implores, "Save our school. Save it now. We've gotta turn this around somehow."

As word spread about this song, the children were invited to perform it at a local TV show. The local Woolworth store started playing the song in the store for shoppers to hear and the Selsted group became a news item in various news networks, including BBC news. At the time that this was all happening, podcasting had grown in popularity and was spreading quite rapidly. It was therefore no surprise that as podcasters learned of the song, they began playing it on their shows. The song was then made available online for download at a mere 99 pence (approximately $1.50 US today). As podcasters across the globe played the song, they directed traffic to the download site. In the US, Adam Curry aired the song on his podcast. He is labeled by some as the Podfather, a podcasting pioneer who drove the use of RSS feeds (a simplified way to subscribe to podcasts), developed by Dave Winer, into the mainstream with his podcast, the Daily Source Code. He launched his show in 2004, but by the time he aired the school's protest song in 2006, he had millions of subscribers, many of whom were podcasting themselves.

Podcasters all over the world played the song, directing more and more traffic to the download site. On the school's website, comments could be found from Canada, the USA, the UK, and other countries. The sentiments shared were very similar: we wish you all the best; we wish you good luck; tell the kids we are all behind them. One podcaster even suggested creating a ringtone for mobile phones as another way to generate funds for the school.

On September 15, two months after the song was first released, a message was posted on the Selsted Primary School webpage. "We have been saved!" The message then goes on to thank a number of people and various media outlets, including Radio Kent, the BBC, and KMFM WOW. There's even a message to podcasters: "To all the podcasters around the world that have taken our small rural school around the world—thanks."

Not only did the song help to keep the school open, the process of doing the song created a powerful space for the children across grade levels to work together as well as learn about media and its role in creating community. They also learned new Discursive practices related to song writing, performing, producing, and marketing. And they learned about the history of their school. The work was therefore cross-curricular, with real-world impact and effect.

A Magical Mystery Tour

A well-known Canadian podcaster, Sylvain Grand'Maison, has previously shared the notion that you are what you hear because he says what you hear affects you, even if there are no visible physical effects (2008). The children whose stories I shared in this chapter were certainly all affected in some way by music, leading them to engage in creating lyrics and/or performing for various reasons in various contexts. Grand'Maison (2008) also notes that musicians know that to become a better musician, you need to play with musicians who are better than you. In their own way, the children apprenticed themselves to musicians whose music appealed to them in some way. Through experiencing varying degrees of music and song, they were able to create music and song for themselves.

Grand'Maison further describes the process of making music as a magical mystery tour whereby the music and sounds produced are not necessarily pre-planned but rather emerge through engagement in the process of being musical, of writing music, of writing songs. This was particularly clear in the case of 3-year-old Elle. Grand'Maison cites an incident that took place on the afternoon of July 6, 1957, when the Quarrymen skiffle group played at the garden fete of St Peter's Church, in Woolton, Liverpool, when John Lennon and Paul McCartney first met. Apparently John Lennon was playing banjo chords on a guitar because he knew how to play and tune a banjo but he did not know how to tune a guitar. He also did not know all the words to the song he was singing, but he knew the chorus, so he made up the verses as he sang. This process is much like the one engaged in by 3-year-old Elle in performing her sunshine love ballad. The idea then of inventing and experimenting with sound and playing with words can have powerful effects. I imagine even more so if framed from a critical literacy perspective. Imagine, then, the potential of using music as a tool for engaging in critical literacies both locally and globally.

Reflection Questions

1. If we believe that part of what we do from a critical literacy perspective is imagine thoughtful ways of thinking about reconstructing and redesigning texts and images to convey different and more socially just and equitable messages, then how might we use what we have learned from Daniella, Jacob, Maisie, and Elle to create opportunities for critical literacies in the music curriculum?
2. One of the key tenets discussed earlier in the book is that from a critical literacy perspective, the world is seen as a socially constructed text that can be read. I note that the earlier students are introduced to this idea, the sooner they are able to understand what it means to be researchers of language and explore ways texts can be revised, rewritten, or reconstructed to shift or reframe the message(s) conveyed. In what ways have you supported your students in engaging as researchers of language who understand what it means to re-construct, disrupt, or reframe texts to create alternate, more socially just versions?

Try This

Earlier on in this chapter, I talked about Mitchell (2016), who layered his lessons by bringing in "music, movement activities, and visual components to help address the multiple intelligences of all students" (p. 272). One strategy that has worked for me while working with both children and adults, as a tool for responding to text, is to have them choose, name, play, and sometimes sing (depending on what they are comfortable doing) a song that best represents what is on their mind with regards to the text. I then ask them to talk about why they chose a particular song.

These discussions have sometimes led to unpacking the songs chosen in ways that make visible the positions from which a person has responded to a text. Once they are able to articulate a position, it is more likely that they will be able to examine that position and re-visit their perspective, thereby creating a space for them to make more informed decisions regarding what they think and understand. In a sense, this is about reading with and/or against a text, but using songs to represent that reading.

9

Critical Literacy, Art, and Everyday Popular Culture Texts

> A critical literacy curriculum needs to be lived. It arises from the social and political conditions that unfold in communities in which we live. As such it cannot be traditionally taught. In other words, as teachers we need to incorporate a critical perspective into our everyday lives with the children we work with in order to find ways to help them understand the social and political issues around them.
>
> (Vasquez, 2004)

In this chapter my intent is to show and tell about creating spaces for engaging in 'pleasurable and powerful critical literacies' (Comber, 2000) with young children, using art, everyday texts, and issues of everyday life. Comber (2000) describes critical literacies as involving people using language to exercise power to enhance everyday life in schools and communities and to question practices of privilege and injustice. Throughout the chapter you will meet children between the ages of 4 and 7 who have participated in doing the kind of critical work that Comber describes.

In a study on the links between everyday popular culture and language arts instruction, Alvermann and Hong Xu (2003) note four approaches to using popular culture in the classroom: treating pop-culture as detrimental to children's development, teaching children to critically analyze popular culture texts, emphasizing the pleasure children take in various forms of media-produced text, and developing children's abilities to be self-reflexive in their uses of popular culture. They state what they feel is problematic with some of these approaches and affirm their endorsement of the fourth approach, developing children's ability to be self-reflexive in their uses of popular culture as an effective way of engaging with popular culture texts. They define self-reflexivity within the context of working with popular culture texts as a way of "striking a balance between teaching [children] to be critical and allowing them to experience pleasures without challenges that can extend their learning" (p. 148).

The question for me is, how can we strike a balance between creating spaces or opportunities for childhood popular culture discourses and everyday texts in the classroom and engage children in working critically with these texts while at the same time making sure not to co-opt their interests? Co-opting their interests refers to taking over such things as popular culture texts about which the children are passionate and turning them into school curriculum, thereby making those texts less desirable. Striking this balance calls for ongoing negotiation of curriculum with children and ongoing observations of what everyday issues and texts are on the minds of children. This negotiation involves constantly listening to what children are talking about, their passions, their interests, and using these to build curriculum that has importance in their lives. There are increasing accounts of such work with children of all ages (Alvermann & Hong Xu, 2003; Comber, 1993; Dyson, 2003; Luke, O'Brien, & Comber, 1994; O'Brien, 1998; Vasquez, 2004).

Everyday Texts: What Are They?

When I use the term 'everyday texts,' I am referring to texts that are spoken or written as part of everyday life, such as newspaper and magazine ads, food wrappers, or television advertisements. These texts can be so common that we do not carefully take notice of them. As a result we can be less aware of the kinds of messages about our world that they convey (Vasquez, 2004). Since these texts are not natural representations of the world, they can be interrogated, deconstructed, and analyzed to uncover the view of the world they represent. In doing so we are able to make visible the lifestyles and social identities that are constructed through what is presented and how it is presented.

Curtis:	You can find 'Gatta Catch 'Em All' in almost all the posters that you find.
Vivian:	Any ideas why that might be?
Curtis:	Uh, I don't know. I can take a guess though.
Vivian:	Okay.
Curtis:	Well, in the show, the object is to catch all the Pokemon. So maybe that 'Gatta Catch 'Em All' means you gotta (pause) catch them all.
Vivian:	So catching, is that the same as or different than collecting?
Emily:	It's sort of like collecting cards.
Miguel:	Except you're collecting the Pokemon.
Emily:	Who wants us to do that?
Miguel:	The sellers?
Curtis:	Ya, they make the Pokemon for their job.

The 4- to 7-year-old children who participated in this conversation raised important issues regarding 'sellers,' 'buyers,' and the consumer world. Evans (2005) looks in more detail at some older children's perceptions of these issues in relation to Beanie Babies. In another publication (Vasquez, 2014a), I did a closer analysis of the conversation that followed this previous exchange whereby I asked the children to look across a series of Pokemon toy packages to find all the words that have to do with collecting. I concluded that it was conversations like this one that set the groundwork for later conversations in which the children and I began to look more closely at the use of words linked to Pokemon texts and how these ideologically positioned readers—that is, how the texts reflect dominant social ideas or beliefs. We did an analysis of the texts by bringing to the fore the way that audience is maintained through the consistent use of the phrase "Gotta Catch 'Em All," as Curtis states, "in almost all the posters (referring to toy packaging, posters, magazines and other Pokemon-related products) you find." We also brought to the fore the notion of consumerism when Emily asked, "Who wants us to do that?" and Miguel replied, "The sellers." We also discovered that the same collecting behavior was encouraged with food items such as Kraft Pokemon Macaroni and Cheese, and Kellogg's Pokemon Cereal. Regarding the macaroni and cheese, for instance, 4-year-old Emily noted, "Instead you don't say 'catch.' It's 'eat.' You 'Gotta Eat 'Em All'." In the same vein, Rula noted, "Like for clothes. You gotta wear them all," referring to the various clothing items that were being manufactured bearing Pokemon characters. Rula's comment regarding clothing led us to further analysis of Pokemon texts, this time with an eye toward constructions of gender.

The Children's Constructions of Gender

Rula: Do you have clothes that are Pokemon?
Miguel: Nah, I don't wear girl stuff, that's gross.
Emily: You have shoes!
Miguel: Shoes aren't clothes, they're just shoes.
Rula: Why? Are clothes girls only?
Miguel: I mean like a pink shirt with Pikachu or something.

Regardless of what Emily and Rula said, Miguel was convinced that Pokemon clothes were for girls only and that Pokemon shoes were for boys. According to its creators, Pokemon are non-gendered and, as such, they should have equal appeal to girls and boys. However, in conversation with the children, it is clear that this is not the case. In order to push the discussion further, I asked the children if they would be interested in designing their own shirts and shoes. The following day, I had prepared sheets of paper with blank T-shirts and shoes to use as templates for their designs. Five-year-old Patrick designed the shirt in Figure 9.1 as a shirt that would most appeal to boys. He said this would be a boy shirt because he drew a Pokemon that had powers that the boys in the class like (referring to the symbols in the circles across the shoulders of the shirt). After seeing many other such designs from some of the other children, Miguel seemed satisfied that boys could wear Pokemon clothing also. He said, "That's funny, I didn't think you could do that. Doh."

Six-year-old Catalina designed the logo to go on a girl's shoe that is seen in Figure 9.2. The logo is a purple unicorn-looking animal with a flowing blond mane. Catalina called the Pokemon logo that she designed 'Colors' and said that it is a horse-type Pokemon. She decided to add to her design a write-up of the Pokemon, saying that her mother's shoes came with a paper about the shoes. She attributes several attacks to Colors: star attack, head butt, yellow

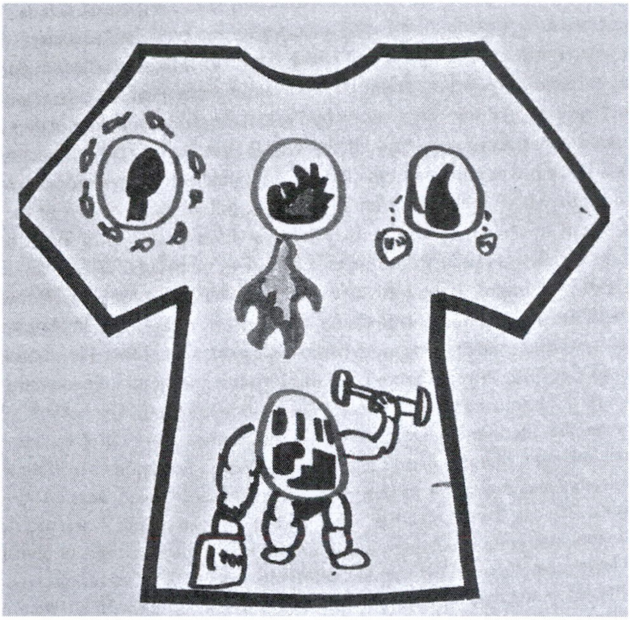

FIG. 9.1 Patrick's Shirt for Boys

FIG. 9.2 Shoe Logo Designed for Girls

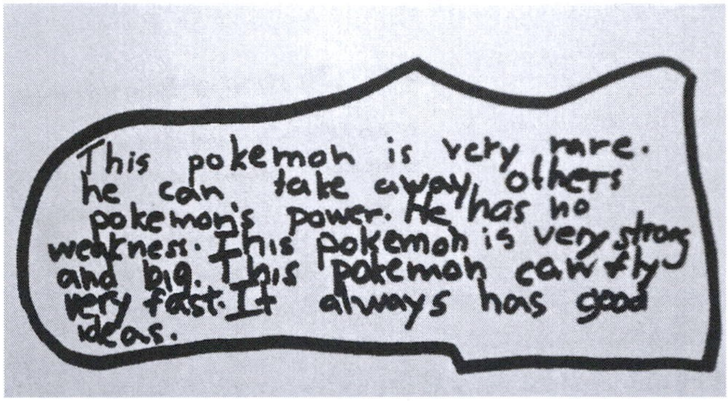

FIG. 9.3 Colors' Attributes

attack, shield attack, and color attack. Attacks are basically a Pokemon's weapons, the ways in which it can beat an opponent in battle. Her write-up, which can be seen in Figure 9.3, was done in a shoe outline. She notes that this Pokemon is very rare and that he can take away other Pokemons' power. She continues by writing, "He has no weakness. This Pokemon is very strong and big. This Pokemon can fly very fast. It always has good ideas."

Re-Design as a Crucial Element in Critical Literacy

Janks (2002) talks about redesign as an element that should be part of any critical literacy work that we do. In our observation regarding gender, simply deconstructing gendered texts such as T-shirts and shoes would not have been enough to offer the children an alternate perspective. Clearly, especially for Miguel, it was not until we designed our own versions of Pokemon shoes and shirts that he realized other alternatives existed, bringing to the fore the notion that texts and images are socially constructed and, as such, they can be deconstructed and re-designed. His statement, "That's funny, I didn't think you could do that. Doh," was his 'aha' moment—that is, his moment of suddenly realizing things could be other than what he originally thought.

Catalina's re-design of a Pokemon shoe was especially interesting to me as she broke down gender stereotypes through her choice of text and image. She began by saying, "This Pokemon is very rare," immediately giving it added value. Earlier on they had talked about specific cards being more desirable, such as the holo cards, which were holographic and not as readily available. At another point in time, the children and I had a discussion regarding which Pokemon they thought were male and which were female and why. What I discovered was that the children looked primarily at the characters' physical attributes to decide on maleness or femaleness. What a character did not look like, e.g. the lack of boy colors, such as blue or green, was also a criterion used to assign gender. Most of the Pokemon that the children claimed to be female were not as powerful or valuable as some of the Pokemon the children claimed to be male. So to say that Colors, who to the other children looked female, was very rare and therefore very valuable, disrupted the schema they had earlier developed for assigning gender. This disruption continued as Catalina wrote that Colors "can take away other Pokemons' power" and that "he has no weakness." Colors, originally thought to be a female by the children, was in fact male according to Catalina. The other children had fully expected, given the way the unicorn looked, that it would be a female, especially since it resembled Lila Unicorn from Barbie of Swan Lake, a popular toy with the girls.

When I asked her why she decided to create a male Pokemon in the way that she did, she basically said that it was because there are lots of ways that males look and lots of ways that females look and that people should not just use how someone looks on the outside to decide what they are really like. She explained, "Just because a boy likes pink, it doesn't mean he isn't strong, or just because a girl likes blue, it doesn't mean she'll beat up other kids." Sharing this with the other children was important as they were able to re-read some of the T-shirts they had previously designed specifically for males or specifically for females. In their re-reading of those shirts, they decided that maybe they needed to think more about the problem with assigning a particular gender to their various T-shirt and shoe designs.

Catalina continued to add value to Colors the Pokemon by describing his strength, saying that he is not only strong but very strong and big too. To put icing on the cake, she finished off by saying that "this Pokemon can move very fast and it always has good ideas."

What we accomplished therefore was to use the principle of re-designing to challenge dominant meanings (Janks, 1993a), which was one way to help the children begin to understand that "texts are constructed from a range of possible options" (p. iii).

After having engaged in designing Pokemon artifacts such as shirts and shoes, the children and I began talking about what it would mean to sell those products. These are the same sorts of questions we might focus on from a media literacy perspective as well. We asked questions like these:

- What would cause someone to want to buy something?
- What kinds of images would be effective?
- What words sound most convincing?
- How do the texts and images in advertising work?
- How can we read these texts with a critical eye so that we are able to make informed decisions about what we buy?
- What leads us to believe a text?
- How can we read between the lines?

These questions may be challenging, but they are important to consider if we are to effectively use everyday texts and issues to create spaces for critical literacy with young children that go beyond simply deconstructing text. Responses to these sorts of questions generate further opportunities for re-designing text thereby re-imagining the way things should be. They enable us, as Luke (1998) suggests, not only to see how the world of texts works in ideological ways, but also to use texts as social tools in ways that allow for a reconstruction of inequitable worlds. In terms of this chapter, art was used as a tool for constructing, re-designing, and representing meaning from a critical literacy perspective. What matters most, however, is that we get started doing some of this important life work—and it is life work because the kinds of literacies that stem from this work are the literacies of everyday life.

Reflection Questions

Consider the following while reflecting on your own practice.

1. What sorts of literacies and/or resources do children bring into the classroom?
2. Where did they appropriate these literacies? In other words, what are the places where these literacies were acquired and how?
3. What literacies are privileged in classrooms? What literacies are ignored? How might we change what literacies are privileged?
4. In what ways does working with everyday texts and issues create spaces for developing literacies that go well beyond that which is mandated in the official curriculum?
5. What role might doing art play in this work?

Try This

The potential for working with the arts or art from a critical literacy perspective are limitless. In fact there are many more examples of children's use of art in this way in other chapters in this book, such as Jessica's creation of her Mountie poster in chapter 3 or Emily's re-designed Fruity Peel-Outs box in chapter 12. I understand, however, that it is not always easy to know where to start. So here is one suggestion for getting started.

First of all, my suggestion is to start where you can, as soon as you can. For instance, you could look at one aspect of toy packaging (the cardboard wrapping around toys or the boxes they come in) or a magazine ad. For instance, one of the toy packages my students analyzed had a gold seal in one corner that had on it, "Increase your intelligence power!" A Pokemon Pop Tarts food package also had a gold seal in the upper right-hand corner. It said, "Limited Edition." A place to start could therefore be to take a similar ad and focus specifically on the seal. When I did this analysis with children, I asked them who they thought would be interested in the words on the seal. Here are some of their responses:

- Teachers because they want [children] to learn.
- Parents because they want their kids to be smart.
- The principal so the school will do good.
- Collectors so they can have a rare collection.
- Kids to be cool because maybe not everyone would have it.
- The guy at the trading card store so he can sell it to someone else for lots of money.

We then talked about the use of gold rather than a basic color and discussed other ways of designing the seal. Would a star shape work differently? What color would be most effective? How might an audience react to a red seal versus a yellow seal or green seal? What shapes would not work as a seal and why?

In your setting, you could have children brainstorm possible audiences and then create their own versions of the seal for those audiences. By doing these kinds of art/design activities, you can begin to create opportunities for looking at how texts are constructed and re-designing texts for particular audiences with an eye toward becoming critical readers of text.

Resource Box 9.1 Engaging With Art From a Critical Literacy Perspective

The following resources can inform ways of engaging with art from a critical literacy perspective. Although some of this work is done with older children, the strategies used could be revised for use with younger children.

Albers, P., Harste, J. C. & Vasquez, V. (2012). Interrupting certainty and making trouble: Teachers' written and visual responses to picturebooks. In P. J. Dunston, L. B. Gambrell, S. K. Fullerton, V. R. Gillis, K. Headley, & P. S. Stecker (Eds.), *60th Yearbook of the National Reading Conference* (pp. 195–201). Oak Creek, WI: NRC.

Albers, P., Harste, J. C., & Vasquez, V. M. (2015). Critical and multimodal literacy curricula. In M. Hamilton, R. Heydon, K. Hibbert, & R. Stooke (Eds), *Negotiating spaces for literacy learning* (pp. 115–130). London, UK: Bloomsbury.

Albers, P., Vasquez, V., & Harste, J. C. (2011). Making visual analysis critical. In D. Lapp & D. Fisher (Eds), *The handbook of research on teaching the English language arts* (pp. 195–201). Mahwah, NJ: Routledge-LA.

Simon, R. (2014). Practitioner inquiry day. *Communities of Inquiry Symposium 2014*. Ethnography Forum at University of Pennsylvania. Available at https://www.youtube.com/watch?v=PBuek2D6DQA

Vasquez, V. M. So the boys won't bother us: Kindergarten students as researchers. Available at https://www.academia.edu/9304302/So_the_Boys_wont_Bother_Us_Kindergarten_Students_as_Researchers

10

Critical Media Literacy

> In today's multimedia world it is insufficient to teach literacy that only addresses traditional concepts of print while ignoring the other major ways we engage with, receive, process, and create images and information . . . In the contemporary era of standardized high-stakes testing and corporate solicitations in public education, the question we must ask is not whether critical media literacy should be taught, but instead, how it should be taught.
>
> (Share, 2015, p. 47)

Share (2015) asks a pivotal question with regards to critical media literacy: How should it be taught? For him there is no doubt that it should be taught, across the curriculum and with learners of all ages. He laments that, unfortunately, "for most of the 54 million students in kindergarten through high school in the U.S., critical media literacy is not an option because it is not available" (Share, 2015, p. 47). In this chapter we venture into the classrooms of two teachers who readily take up the challenge of creating spaces for their students to explore critical media literacy. Both are teachers from Canada; Bryan Woods teaches pre-kindergarten and kindergarten and David Chiola-Nakai teaches sixth grade. We also venture into a classroom I shared with a group of kindergarten students. All of us worked with diverse groups of students in schools located in a suburb of Toronto, Ontario.

A *Nike* Story: Pairing Media Texts With Texts Written for Children

Teacher:	What are the "uniforms" that kids wear in school?
Victor:	What do you mean?
Teacher:	Well, what kinds of clothes do cool kids wear? How do we know when someone is "cool"?
Tomislav:	Cool kids wear Nike.
Others:	Nike is the best. Yeah! Nike rules!

The previous conversation took place in David Chiola-Nakai's sixth-grade classroom in a Catholic school in the greater Toronto area of Ontario, Canada. The class was comprised of a very diverse group of 32 sixth-grade students. Like my kindergarten students and me, David Chiola-Nakai and his sixth-grade students also worked with multimodal texts, combining books written for children with everyday texts and media texts as one way to create space for critical literacy. The above conversation was part of a discussion following a read-aloud of *The Hockey Story* by R. J. Childerhose (1981). The story is about a hockey game between a team from an urban area and one from a rural area. David's students were immediately drawn to the obvious difference between the two teams' uniforms. The team from the city wore matching uniforms and was outfitted from helmet to skates. The team from the rural area wore a ragtag mix of whatever equipment and uniforms they could gather from their neighborhood. This contrast in the resources available to each team led David, together with his students, to discuss inequity and the ways that people can position one another in classist ways, including judging someone based on the clothes he or she wears. As part of that conversation, they discussed what clothing is considered "cool" and wondered who determines what is cool. The preceding conversation took place as part of the discussion on this topic.

Bigelow, Christensen, Karp, Miner, and Peterson (1994) state "if we ask students to critique the world but then fail to encourage them to act, our classrooms can degenerate into factories for cynicism" (p. 4). In other words, to critique void of action does not lead to change. The only thing it can lead to is the creation of cynics who talk about what is wrong with the world without contributing to changing that world. David recognized that he could capitalize on his students' interest in Nike to engage in critical literacy that could lead to some sort of social action. This is consistent with Chavanu's (2016) contention that "media literacy can play a necessary role in helping our students become critically literate and reactive to the powerful influence of television, video games, commercial advertising, popular magazines, and movies" (p. 22).

However, the following exchange took place even before he could begin to address the notion of taking action in the world to change inequitable ways of being.

Tomislav:	But Nike is all over the world. How can we make a change?
Victor:	We could stop buying their products.
Mike:	I'll never stop buying Nike!

It became clear to David that engaging in critical literacy work could cause tension in the classroom. Some of his students were clearly expressing anti-corporate agenda sentiments, while others treasured the cultural capital that came with being a Nike wearer and embodying the name brand. Finding comfort in the notion that tension is a great propeller of learning, David forged on regardless of the tensions he began to face regarding how to enact a critical media literacy curriculum.

Using Tensions to Propel Learning

> A social system can only be held in place by the meanings the people make of it. Culture is deeply inscribed in the differential distribution of power within a society, for power relations can only be stabilized or destabilized by the meanings that people make of them. Culture is a struggle for meanings as society is a struggle for power.
>
> (Fiske, 1989, p. 20)

According to Fiske (1989), a social system or a society's accepted ways of being are maintained through use. The important question is, who decides on what systems to maintain and use and for what purposes? Who gets to do what, however, is rooted in who has or does not have power to act in particular ways. Fiske refers to this as a differential distribution of power. David wondered how Fiske's notion of the differential distribution of power intersected with the issue of classism and inequity his students had raised. He realized that not acting on these issues in some way or at least making visible to his students possible ways of taking action would mean that he and his students would be contributing to maintaining inequitable ways of being.

While attempting to figure out how to deal with his students' struggle for meaning, David mentioned their conversation regarding Nike to one of his colleagues, who proceeded to tell him about a television report on Nike's mistreatment of factory workers in developing countries. In response, David asked if she would talk to his class and share what she had seen. At that time, he had not realized the generative nature of connecting everyday text such as the television segment on Nike with the original conversations regarding equity in *The Hockey Story* (Childerhose, 1981).

> David: I began to sense my students' growing awareness of the overwhelming presence Nike had in their lives. They began to take much more notice of the plethora of Nike gear worn in the school. I heard disbelief in their voices as they began to discuss issues of fair wages and child labor and the role that we play as consumers in maintaining children as laborers when we consume Nike products. Posters appeared on the classroom walls depicting anti-Nike sentiments. Similar to the way it has come to dominate the sports world, the Nike sports empire suddenly became the focus of a classroom study.
>
> I could feel the sense of being overwhelmed by the idea of taking on such a huge conglomerate. Imagine a group of 11- to 12-year-old students taking on the giant of the sports world. But as Harste (1997) has said, history is replete with examples of "tripping the giant."
>
> (p. 2)

What started as a conversation about a children's book turned into a discussion around issues of power and consumerism when the issues raised in the book were paired with the inequities made visible in a television segment.

Creating Spaces for Students to Think Differently

David: I started to see how the classroom could offer space for analyzing the daily texts that students bring to school. I realized that spaces for conversation on social issues could come from an assortment of texts, not just books. I think I was beginning to further my understanding of interrogating texts and how to make them problematic. I could also see how the classroom was becoming a safe zone for my students to critically analyze the world around them. Not everyone took the same position. Many remained loyal to Nike and refused to stop wearing the brand name's clothing or shoes. Others engaged in a personal boycott, stripping their bodies of any sort of Nike wear to symbolize their protest against the corporation's treatment of their workers.

David found himself caught in the whirlwind of events happening in and out of the classroom. His role became blurred as he found himself in the position of both a resource and a learner. He searched the papers and magazines to provide articles and materials to support his students' inquiries and found new ways of using existing learning tools and strategies.

David: I began to see how we could use surveys and graphing, investigating maps and charts, money, letter writing, learning logs, posters, questionnaires, response logs, and presentations in our investigations. For example, two students designed a survey to find out the approximate number of hats, shoes, and shirts that were owned by students in our school and how many of these were Nike products. They took the information and drew graphs and reported what they had discovered to the rest of the class to show the predominance of Nike consumers. They then went on to do a presentation to our reading buddies, first-grade students with whom we read

> picture books once a week, about Nike's mistreatment of workers. I found this helped my students to articulate their concerns better while disseminating information they thought was important.

Many students designed posters depicting anti-Nike sentiment. These were alternate versions of existing Nike ads. Two other students wrote a joint letter to Phillip Knight, CEO of Nike at the time, asking him to tell Nike's side of the story on the use of child laborers and the use of sweatshops.

Comber (2001c) notes,

> Children are accustomed to thinking analytically about power and pleasure. . . . The task for teachers is to help children to develop a meta-awareness and a meta-language for what they already know how to do and to assist them in applying these resources to the texts and situations of school life. The varying practices that different children bring with them can become part of a collective capacity to solve problems and approach possibilities.
>
> (p. 2)

Developing a collective capacity to solve problems and approach possibilities is one of the goals that David had hoped could be accomplished through the class inquiry. The point of the inquiry was not to make people change their minds but to provide students with new ways of talking and thinking about "the everyday worlds of community, media, and literature" (Comber, 2001c, p. 2) for them to make informed critical decisions.

Critical Media Literacy and Young Children

Bryan Woods also made use of multi-media text sets in his combined pre-kindergarten and kindergarten classroom. Here is his response when asked to describe his students.

> This past year the class was diverse on many fronts. The classroom was made up of 25 students—16 SK [Senior Kindergarten] students and 9 JK [Junior Kindergarten or pre-Kindergarten] students. Of these students there was a range of diverse family cultural backgrounds. Half of my students' families were of the Muslim faith and coming from Middle Eastern countries. I had a few students who were born in India or Asian countries who spoke Urdu at home and were of Hindi faith. As well, I had a few

families that were from the Caribbean. Out of the 25 students, 1/2 were born in Canada and 2/3 spoke another language at home.

Students were from a range of socio-economic lower to middle class demographics. Some families rented basement apartments while other students lived in large affluent detached homes. Many families had grandparents living in the same household. Also, there was a wide range of academic strengths as well.

Two students turned 4 in September while several SK students are turning 6 in January. As an educator, stretching these children into new spaces was at times a challenge as this was a first experience in a "formal" learning environment for 7 of the 9 JK students who had not attended an early years, program.

Within the class setting, I was privileged to work with three students with learning exceptionalities. One student, Kayhan was a student that was non-verbal autistic. Kayhan was a student that would often run out of the classroom. We had to explore many new ways of reaching Kayhan from daily and frequent use of video, technology and movement learning opportunities. We made it a priority to involve the parents into his daily school experience through Skyping, video recordings, daily emails and texts. As well, I had a student David who has Down Syndrome. Some of the same strategies that we used for Kayhan applied to David. Lastly, I was able to work with a gifted student, Isabella. She was extremely motivated in activities that involved reading with texts and reading against texts, technology opportunities through making videos, slideshows, podcasts, blogging, etc. She regularly wanted to discuss, write and read from multiple ways of knowing and perspectives in math, picture books, media articles, videos and social issues going on in our classroom and in the school.

Working with such a diverse group of students energized Bryan. He found pleasure in finding new and different ways to ensure that he was supporting each of his students' learning. He also made it a point to challenge them and treat them as intelligent, capable learners. Such was the case when he and his students had a conversation about Father's Day.

Bryan: I showed two ads this morning side by side and we discussed what they noticed that was different between the "two dads ad" and the "stereotypical, [heterosexual] hallmark ad."

The two ads Bryan referred to were included in Father's Day flyers that were circulated in the community where his students lived. One ad for Ridemakerz depicts a woman, a man, a young boy, and a young girl. The caption for the ad reads, "Build memories with Dad," referring to building remote control cars with Dad, which is the product the ads are marketing. This is made clear by the image which shows the adult male (Dad), the boy and the girl each holding a car, while the adult female (Mom) smiles standing behind the three. The second ad, a JC Penney advertisement, depicts two men with a young girl and a young boy. The caption for this ad was "first pals." In the ad one man is being hugged by the little girl while the second man is hugging the little boy. In both ads, smiles could be seen on everyone's faces. The text in the ad reads:

> "First Pals: What makes Dad so cool? He's the swim coach, tent maker, best friend, bike fixer and hug giver—all rolled into one. Or two."

The text at the bottom reads:

> "Real-life dads, Todd Koch and Cooper Smith with their children Claire and Mason."

Like David, Bryan also experienced conflicting viewpoints shared by his students.

> Bryan: We explored and the kids said that the two men were dads and those were their kids, we discussed how do we know, could they be brothers, cousins, uncles etc. When I said what if I was to tell you that the two men are married or in love, and then a few reactions surfaced. One JK girl said, "Boys marry girls."

> We discussed this point as a group:

> I said is that ok if these two men are married? Why do people become married? If this is a family about love, caring and family . . . then should it matter if boys marry boys and girls marry girls . . . they all seem to agree no it didn't matter.

When asked about his curricular goals, Bryan said that he tried to introduce critical literacy into all areas of the curriculum and into the routine habits and lives of his students and their parents:

> Even when working with 3–5 year olds, I want them to learn to question the 'everyday normal,' which is represented by the

> heterosexual couple in the Ridemakerz advertisement. I wanted to have my students' parents as co-teachers. To this end I use a vast array of technology. I shared information daily through Twitter, emails and a class blog. I also Skype with parents, send video-texts, and audio recordings. I want parents to feel like they are relevant members of the classroom and feel included in critical classroom discourse.

Bryan shared that the discussions he had with his students about rethinking Father's Day and disrupting the stereotypes that shape that day was one of his top three most successful critical literacy focused studies. I imagine his openness and transparency with the parents had much to do with his being able to carve out space in the curriculum for engaging in this kind of important media literacy work. This instance represents the kind of ongoing work that Bryan does with young children in deconstructing and reconstructing texts in their everyday worlds.

In the next section of this chapter, I will focus on the technical characteristics of visual images, their social functions, the context of text images, and what this type of critical analysis might look like in classrooms.

The Concept of Offer and Demand

Halliday (1978) describes four basic functions of speech as offering information, offering goods and services, demanding information, and demanding goods and services. Kress and van Leeuwen (2006) have taken this concept of offer and demand and applied it to visual images. In this section, we return to my kindergarten classroom to have a look at what this concept might look like when used with a piece of everyday text.

One of the artifacts brought to the classroom by one of my students was a *Kids Tribute* magazine, a publication dedicated to children about current movies for young people. A Pokemon ad in the magazine particularly caught our attention because it took up two side-by-side pages. On the right side, a group of Pokemon is portrayed entering into some sort of arena or stadium. The image is similar to the entrance of players during professional sporting events such as basketball, football, or hockey. The ad is for Pokemon Stadium, which is a video game. It is billed as "the Pokemon battle you've been waiting for . . . the way Pokemon were meant to battle." The people in the stands are made to appear as though they are cheering for the entering Pokemon in the same way that sports fans cheer for their favorite teams and players. Using this ad, one of the things that could be focused on is the relationship in Western society between power and being a professional athlete and how this is being connected to what it means to be a Pokemon trainer. For now, however, I would like to focus on the concept of 'offer and demand' as it pertains to this particular image.

Kress and van Leeuwen (2006) talk about the fundamental difference between pictures where the participants in the image, the characters—in this case, the Pokemon—look directly at the readers' eyes and pictures where this is not the case. They state "when represented participants look directly at the viewer, vectors, formed by participants' eyelines, connect the participants with the viewer. Contact is established even if it is only on an imaginary level" (p. 122).

Using Kress and van Leeuwen's strategy, I made an overhead of the double-page ad, which I projected on the classroom wall. Together, the children and I drew lines from each of the characters' eyes, enabling us to have a closer look at where the vectors formed by their eyelines would end. Having done this, it was clear that the characters—Pikachu, Meowth, Psycluck, Poliwhirl, Venusaur, Blastoise, and Charizard—gaze directly toward us, the viewers. One of the characters, Charizard, was positioned in the ad as flying over the other Pokemon. This visual effect helps with the illusion that the Pokemon are coming toward the viewer, therefore maintaining the Pokemons' contact with the viewer.

Kress and van Leeuwen also state that there can be "vectors, formed by a gesture in the same direction" (2006, p. 22). In the ad Pikachu, Meowth, Poliwhirl, Venusaur, Blastoise, and Charizard all have one arm back and one arm with a forward vector. This is seen more clearly in an ad for Pokemon puzzles in which Ash is holding a Pokeball directly at the viewer, and even more clearly in a Super Mario figure located in the bottom left-hand corner on the left side of the double-page spread. This gesture is reminiscent of "We Want YOU" US Armed Forces recruitment posters. The children and I looked at this gesture in a number of ads and also tried doing the gesture ourselves. We also then posed with our arms stretched out in different directions and talked about which ones most effectively made the viewers feel as though they were being asked to participate. Curtis even went as far as to create his own Pokemon stadium out of clay in order to play with the idea of gestures and how audience is constructed (Figure 10.1).

The configuration of the participants' gaze and hand gesture functions in particular ways. First, the visual formation used creates

FIG. 10.1 Pokemon Stadium

direct address. A visual 'you' is formed through this address whereby an image is designed in a way that indicates to the reader, "I am talking to you." Secondly, the producer of the image uses it to do something to the viewer. Kress and van Leeuwen refer to this kind of image as a demand (2006, p. 123). They state that the participant's gaze (and the gesture, if present) demands something from the viewer, "demands that the viewer enter into some kind of imaginary relation with him or her" (p. 122). The image, through the use of gaze and gesture, signifies a "Hey you, I mean you, join me in battle, play with me, buy me and you will be powerful too" kind of relationship. So "when images demand, what they are demanding are the goods and services that realize a particular social relation" (Kress & van Leeuwen, 2006, p. 129). In this case, one relationship is that of producer and consumer. As such the visual image defines the viewer. Knowing this, important questions to be asked include: What does this ad say I can and cannot be? What does this ad say I can and cannot do?

These questions are akin to the basic underlying question asked of any text from a critical literacy perspective: What is this text trying to do to me? In the Nike story, David and his students work to unpack the ways in which Nike works to position consumers in particular ways in order to help them to find ways to think differently. Bryan and his pre-kindergarten students explored ways that Father's Day advertisements worked to put on offer particular versions of family. Through ongoing conversation with the children and through sharing those conversations with the parents, Bryan was able to create spaces to begin to disrupt the stereotypes associated with Father's Day. In my work with the kindergarten children, the underlying question we asked was how print ads work to create a producer/consumer relationship. Through technical analysis of a Pokemon advertisement, we worked to unpack how this relationship is created.

These everyday texts surround us to the point where they can go by unnoticed. How might you create spaces in your classroom to make sure that these sorts of texts are noticed, critically read, analyzed, deconstructed, and re-designed as a way to build a more informed citizenry who understand the way that texts work to produce particular effects that privilege some over others?

Reflection Questions

1. Make a list of everyday texts you can find in your community along with the everyday texts your students bring to the classroom (magazines, ads, posters and cards, T-shirt logos, logos on backpacks, lunch bags, and so forth). How might you use these materials in combination with children's books to create curricular activities and materials?
2. Linger with one of the everyday texts that you found. How might you support your students to redesign problematic notions of the text? How might you design an alternate version from a different, more equitable perspective?

Try This

1. Reading text sets (see Resource Box 10.1 at the end of this chapter) on a particular topic can help students to understand that texts are never neutral, and that they are constructed by particular people with particular goals and motivations (Comber, 2001b). A text set is a group of books and other print and media materials such as magazine articles and video clips designed to support the study of a particular theme, genre, or

issue. A set usually consists of at least four or five texts and should be carefully constructed to provide different perspectives. Sometimes these perspectives are complementary and other times they may be conflicting; nevertheless, they offer a way of viewing the same area under study. In the case of the Nike inquiry, David's students learned to read between the lines of Nike ads as well as media reports on Nike's corporate practices, which all started from the inequities that his students noticed in a story about a hockey game.

- What media texts are of interest to your students? How might you find out?
- Once you have an idea of what they might be interested in exploring, create a text set by pulling together multimodal resources that would be useful in helping them to make critically informed decisions with regards to the particular topic or issue.

2. Return to Bryan's story. What other things might he have done with his students, building from their comments or further analyzing the ads? For instance, in the ad with the two dads, what effect does the phrase "real life dad" have on how we might read the ad? What might have been the reasoning behind using such a phrase? What questions might you ask of the ad in which the mom is in the background while the dad and children are positioned in the foreground?

Resource Box 10.1 Media Literacy Resources

Alvermann, D. E., Moon, J. S., & Hagood, M. C. (1999). *Popular culture in the classroom: Teaching and researching critical media literacy*. Newark, DE: International Reading Association; Chicago: National Reading Conference.

Buckingham, D. (1993). *Children talking television: The making of television literacy*. London: Routledge Falmer.

Buckingham, D., & Sefton-Green, J. (1995). *Cultural studies goes to school: Reading and teaching popular media*. London: Taylor & Francis.

Evans, J. (2005). *Literacy moves on: Popular culture, new technologies, and critical literacy in the elementary classroom*. Portsmouth, NH: Heinemann.

Gee, J. P. (2003). *What video games have to teach us about learning and literacy*. New York: Palgrave Macmillan.

Guernsey, L., & Levine, M. H. (2015). *Tap, click, read: Growing readers in a world of screens*. New York: Jossey-Bass.
Kavanagh, K. (1997). *Texts on television: School literacies through viewing in the first years of school*. Adelaide, South Australia: Department of Education and Children's Services.
Klein, N. (2000). *No logo: Taking aim at the brand bullies*. Toronto, ON: Vintage Canada.
Lankshear, C., & Knobel, M. (2007). *A new literacies sampler*. New York: Peter Lang.
Marsh, J. (2005). (Ed.) *Popular culture, new media and digital literacy in early childhood*. New York: Routledge Falmer.
Medina, C. L., & Wohlwend, K. E. (2014). *Literacy, play and globalization: Converging imaginaries in children's critical and cultural performances*. New York: Routledge.
Scheibe, C. L., & Rogow, F. (2011). *The teacher's guide to media literacy: Critical thinking in a multimedia world*. New York: Corwin.
Share, J. (2015). *Media literacy is elementary: Teaching Youth to critically read and create media. Second edition* (Rethinking Childhood). New York: Peter Lang.
Wohlwend, K. E. (2013). Literacy playshop: New literacies, popular media, and play in the early childhood classroom. New York: Teachers College Press.

Resource Box 10.2 Learning More About Text Sets

Harste, J. C., Leland, C., Lewison, M., Ociepka, A., & Vasquez, V. (2000). Supporting critical conversations in classrooms. In K. M. Pierce (Ed.), *Adventuring with books: A booklist for Pre-K–Grade 6* (12th ed., pp. 507–512). Urbana, IL: National Council of Teachers of English.
Leland, C., Harste, J. C., Ociepka, A., Lewison, M., & Vasquez, V. (1999). Exploring critical literacy: You can hear a pin drop. *Language Arts*, 77(1), 70–77.
Short, K. G., Harste, J. C., & Burke, C. L. (1996). *Creating classrooms for authors and inquirers*. Portsmouth, NH: Heinemann.
Vasquez, V., Tate, S. L., & Harste, J. C. (2013). Negotiating critical literacies with te*achers*. New York: Routledge.

11

Critical Literacy and New Technologies

Scarlett: Hi! My name is Scarlett. You might remember me from the musical last week. This week we will tell you about how we're going to save money for the trip to the Baltimore Aquarium in Baltimore, Maryland, USA. We will tell the story of how we are doing this.

[¡Hola! Me llamo Scarlett. Puede ser que me recuerdas de la parte musical de la semana pasada. Esta semana les vamos a contar sobre como vamos a ahorrar dinero para el excursión al Acuario de Baltimore en Baltimore, Maryland, USA. Vamos a contarle el cuento de cómo vamos hacer esto.]

Ben: Hi! My name is Ben and this is how it began. Our class had a meeting about the trips of the year. Scarlett was the one that asked if we were going to go to the Baltimore Aquarium this year. Ms. Maggie, our teacher, told us we could not go because it costs too much money. We didn't agree with our teacher. Then I said we could sell things to save money for the trip.

[¡Hola! ¡Mi nombre es Ben y esto es como empezó! Nuestra clase tuvo una reunión sobre las excursiones del año. Scarlett fue la que preguntó si íbamos a ir al Acuario de Baltimore este año. Nuestra maestra Sra. Maggie nos dijo que no podíamos ir porque cuesta demasiado dinero. Nosotros no estuvimos de acuerdo con nuestra maestra. Entonces yo dije que podíamos vender cosas para ahorrar el dinero para la excursión.]

Scarlett: We decided to have a meeting with [the principal]. We sent him a letter via e-mail and took a copy to his office. He gave us an appointment for Friday. We believe that the meeting was good. Then we started to prepare all the hard work. We cannot wait to see what will happen tomorrow.

[Decidimos de tener una reunión con (el director de la escuela). Le mandamos una carta por correo electrónico y llevamos una copia a su oficina. El nos dio una cita para el viernes. Pensamos que la reunión era buena. Entonces empezamos a preparar todo el trabajo duro que íbamos hacer todo este año. Otra vez hicimos carteles y enseñamos a nuestros compañeros como hacerlos. Esta vez más clases participaron. No podemos esperar para ver lo que va a pasar mañana.]

A Podcast Is Born

The opening exchange represents how the children in Carol Felderman's second-grade classroom used podcasting as a tool for conveying messages about projects they were doing or for sharing their thinking on topics or issues that were important to them, both locally, such as advocating for certain privileges, and globally, such as global warming or environmental issues. A podcast is an on-demand Internet broadcast or show that is either in audio or video format. "On demand" refers to the portability of the show; listeners can listen or watch using their desktop or laptop computer or upload the show onto their digital player or other mp3 listening device that organizes and plays audio or video files. Listeners can also subscribe to a podcast so that they can receive new shows as they are released. Releasing a show refers to making it public so that others can listen.

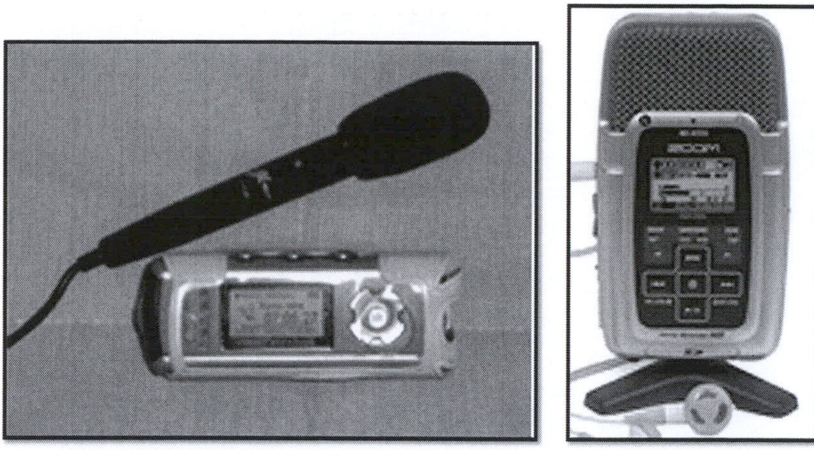

FIG. 11.1 Digital Recording Devices

Carol and her second graders took on the role of podcasters during the spring of 2007. A podcaster, the person(s) doing the podcast, records either audio or video of themselves or others, using a digital recorder (see Figure 11.1) and then uploads it, or posts it, to a place on the Internet for others to hear or view. Most modern laptops have built-in sound cards, which allow you to use inexpensive microphones to record directly into the computer using software such as Audacity (www.audacity.sourceforge.net) or Garageband (www.apple.com/ilife/garageband/). The quality of the recording is not as good as using an external recorder, but the quality improves with the use of a better microphone. Another option is to use a recording device with a USB interface to the computer. Recordings are done directly into the computer using software as noted previously. The quality of the recordings is remarkably better than using the built-in sound cards. (Refer to Table 11.1 for steps to subscribe to a podcast and Figure 11.1 for recommended recording devices.)

In their show, the second graders often included Spanish because a good number of the children in the school were native Spanish speakers learning English, and many of those who were native English speakers were in the Spanish Immersion program. The dual-language episodes made the messages being conveyed by the children more accessible to Spanish-speaking members of the school community and their families.

TABLE 11.1
Subscribing to a Podcast

Steps	Procedure
Step 1	Install a podcatcher (podcast receiver in which you can download podcasts for listening and/or viewing). There are several choices that are available for free. Two of the most popular are iTunes and Juice. Both of these can be used with Windows (PC) or Macintosh (Apple) units. Free Podcatchers: iTunes: www.apple.com/itunes/ jpodder: sourceforge.net/projects/jpodder juice: juicereceiver.sourceforge.net/ myPodder: www.podcastready.com/ Or go to the Podcatcher Matrix site (www.podcatchermatrix.org/), where you can compare a number of different systems to decide on which one best suits your needs.
Step 2	Once you have installed a podcatcher, copy the link from the RSS feed of the show (RSS is a format for delivering web content that changes regularly as in podcasts that release new shows on an ongoing basis). This is usually an orange button marked XML or RSS.
Step 3	Paste the link into your podcatching client. Once you have completed steps 1–3, new shows on podcasts to which you have subscribed will download automatically whenever you ask your podcatcher to update your files. There is no limit to the number of podcasts to which you can subscribe.

The sign in Figure 11.2, which was prominently displayed in Carol's second-grade classroom, attests to how the children felt about taking on podcasting as a new communicative practice, or way of communicating events, thoughts, and ideas.

Comber, Nixon, and Reid (2007) note that in the teaching of literacy, our role as teachers includes extending the repertoires of literacy and communications practices available to our students. They claim what we need is a pedagogy of responsibility, which is about "classroom practice that is informed and structured by teachers' commitment to engaging with questions of diversity and democracy"

FIG. 11.2 Podcast Sign

(p. 14) with their students. Place-based pedagogies, they say, foreground the local and the known and are opportunities for teachers "to structure learning and communication experiences around the things that are most meaningful to their students: their own places, people and popular cultures, and concerns" (p. 14). They ask how technology, such as sending a message or text using a cell phone, creating a video, or participating in online spaces such as electronic art galleries for children provide new and interesting ways for children to communicate their ideas, questions, and understanding about the world around them. Comber and her colleagues further note,

> Literacy teaching cannot, and we believe it should not, be a content-free zone. We know that there is great potential for students to expand their literate repertoires when they become deeply engaged in acquiring new knowledge about things that matter.
> (p. 14)

There is a line in the movie *Cars* (Lasseter & Ranft, 2006) in which Sally, one of the main characters, reflects on a time when roads and roadways moved with the land rather than cutting through it. She specifically refers to the famous Route 66. She lamented that back then, "Cars didn't drive on the road to make great time; they drove on the road to have a great time." In pedagogies of responsibility and place as described by Comber, Nixon, and Reid (2007), the journey matters. This chapter focuses on a journey into the world of podcasting by a group of second graders and the transformative effects that resulted from the experience. As part of this, I will explore the ways in which this new technological tool intersects with critical literacy.

New Technologies as Tools for Engaging in Critical Literacy Work

In Chapter 1, I included a set of tenets through which I engage with critical literacies in the classroom. These are the same tenets I attempt to share with other teachers in my conversations with them regarding creating spaces for critical literacy in their settings. The tenet, which refers to text design, production, critique and transformation, is really where new technologies and social media could have a strong role. Text design and production refers to the creation or construction of texts and the decisions that are part of that process. This includes the notion that it is not good enough to simply create texts for the sake of "practicing a skill." If children are to create texts, they ought to be able to let those texts do the work intended. For instance, if children are doing surveys or petitions, they ought to be done with real-life intent for the purpose of dealing with a real issue. If children write petitions, they ought to be able to send them to the person for whom they were intended. Helping children understand real-life functions of text is an important component of growing as a literate individual.

Lankshear and Knobel (2007) ask the question, "What can new technologies afford literacy work in schools?" In this chapter I am particularly concerned with the question, "What can new technologies and social media afford our work with critical literacy?" Social media tools such as podcasting and blogging allow people to connect electronically using the Internet. *Social media* refers to the integration of technology and social interaction online.

This question, of what new technologies afford the work we do, rings especially true in the area of text design (creating written, drawn, or electronic texts), or redesign (taking existing texts, critiquing their construction, and then creating new texts), and production (producing or constructing texts). I want to be clear that in and of itself, the use of new technologies and social media does not constitute engagement with critical literacies. Just because one is using new technology in the classroom does not mean one is simultaneously engaging in critical literacies. Rather, these new technologies and social media can be used as tools within our critical literacy work. Such tools can be used in the production of texts and also in the distribution of texts both locally and globally.

The potential impact of using new technologies to make accessible to others the work we do is astounding. For instance, researchers at The Diffusion Group, a consumer technology research and marketing firm, predicted that the US podcast audience will climb from 840,000 in 2005 to 56 million by 2010 (The Diffusion Group, 2005). More recently, Libsyn, a podcast hosting site, reported having experienced 2.6 billion podcast downloads in 2014 alone. What started out as a system for distributing homespun radio programming over the Internet has caught on with big media companies such as ABC News, NBC News, ESPN Disney, and National Public Radio, who all have podcast programming. comScore Inc., a global Internet information provider that maintains databases regarding ways in which the Internet is used and the wide variety of activities that are occurring online, reported that in December 2008, the Internet surpassed one billion global users (Gavin, 2009). By 2014 this number grew to over three billion global users. This statistic refers only to individual users and does not include those who use Internet cafés or computers in public settings such as libraries. Given these statistics, it's not a surprise that the Oxford University Press (2005) selected *podcast* as Word of Year in 2005. It competed against words like *trans fat* and *bird flu* (www.us.oup.com/us/brochure/NOAD_podcast/).

Also, given the proliferation of computer access around the globe, it is important to consider the question of whether children of the 21st century are disadvantaged when they are not given opportunities to grow at least some understanding of the ways in which new technologies can be used to do particular kinds of work in our everyday lives and how such technology impacts our lives. This is particularly important in places where hardware and software is readily available. The shame of the matter is that access to the hardware and software is not the primary problem. The major issues lie in the lack of training for using technology and in particular opportunities for teachers to imagine the role technology could play in their curriculum, not as an add-on but as an integral part.

New Technical Stuff and New Ethos Stuff

What new things can we do, in terms of literacy teaching and learning, with the use of technology, and what can we do differently in our teaching as a result? In terms of thinking about possible affordances, a differentiation between Web1.0 and Web2.0 is useful (see Table 11.2 for examples of Web1.0 and Web2.0 software). In the Web1.0 world, information flows in one direction. Webpages, for instance, are static and only allow the viewing or reading of content

TABLE 11.2
Examples of Web1.0 and Web2.0 Software

Examples of Use	Web1.0 One-way flow of information	Web2.0 Interactive software that allows a user to participate in open sharing of content through various social networking tools on the Internet.
Photographs	Kodak Gallery (Ofoto) www.kodakgallery.com	Flickr www.flickr.com/
Reference	Britannica Online www.britannica.com	Wikipedia www.wikipedia.com
Content Organization	Personal webpage	Blog

on the page. Blogs, on the other hand, in a Web2.0 world allow users to participate in open sharing of content through various social networking tools on the Internet. Networking tools like Flickr (www.flickr.com) allow users to not only share photos but also organize, link to other Flickr users' photos, comment on one's own and others' photos, and assign various levels of copyright to photos so that they can be used by other web users. Photos can also be tagged, meaning they can be categorized, so that they are "discoverable" (formerly referred to as *searchable*) on the Internet. Readers also are encouraged to comment on blog posts and share links to other related sites. What this does is create a stronger presence for the blogger or user of social networking tools. A strong presence draws more traffic to a blog site, making information being shared much more accessible and widespread. In their differentiation, Lankshear and Knobel (2007) use the terms *new technical stuff* and *new ethos stuff*. New technical stuff refers to living in a digital culture, or digitality, and what that affords: connectivity, social networking, and instant information. The new ethos stuff refers to a shift of mindset, or way of thinking about technology use, as a result of the new technical stuff.

In terms of podcasting, the focus of this chapter, the question here is, "What does podcasting afford the work done by the second graders?" Said differently, what sorts of possibilities for connecting with the world outside the classroom are made available through the use of this social networking tool and specifically, how might this tool be used in carrying out their critical literacy work?

Podcasting With Second Graders: Getting Started

Carol Felderman's second-grade students were born into a world that is technologically very different from the world she and I were born into. The statistics I shared earlier regarding the number of Internet users today attests to this. It was not surprising, therefore, that many of the children came to school with knowledge of and experience with the new technological stuff and new ethos stuff described by Lankshear and Knobel (2007). Their interest in podcasting was, therefore, not a surprise.

The second-grade classroom is located in a school with more than 800 students. According to the school website, the students represent more than 40 countries of origin and more than 20 different languages spoken at home, although the dominant of these is Spanish. The neighborhood is located about 25 minutes outside of Washington, DC, in a neighborhood that is experiencing increased gang activity and where most of the children receive free or reduced-cost lunch. On average there were 20 students in the class. Fifty percent of the children were English-language learners. Sixty-five percent received free or subsidized meals. There was one student identified with learning disabilities and another eight in referral process for identification as learning disabled. This was a complex mix of children with varied needs.

It was after the second graders heard Carol's voice in a segment she did for the Critical Literacy in Practice Podcast (www.clippodcast.com), which I host, that the children first started asking questions about podcasting. Carol shared their curiosity with me, after which time I sent her links from children who were podcasting, such as "Halloween Boy" and the "Children of Selsted." The "Halloween Boy" podcast was done by an 8-year-old boy who shares topics that are interesting to him. In his show, he shares stories he retells or that he has made up himself along with tips, such as how to make bubbles. The "Children of Selsted" is the story of the school community in chapter 8 that wrote a song to keep their school open. Hearing other children's voices through the Internet generated more interest and conversation. It was one of these conversations that led to the children's desire to start a podcast of their own.

100% Kids: Podcasting and Identity Work

After much deliberation, the children decided they wanted to share on the podcast those issues they had been taking up that focus on fairness and injustice, not to take the moral high ground but to make accessible to potential listeners—both kids and adults—how they have attempted to contribute to change in different spaces and places. Following further conversation, they decided to call their show *100% Kids* to indicate that they (the children) would generate the topics to be discussed on the show and that the voices you would hear on the show would primarily be theirs. Some of the topics they addressed in their show include animal rights, global/environmental issues, being positioned as powerless (as in the decision to cancel a school trip that the second graders had been excited to attend), and dealing with identity work (such as the ways in which some of the children who were hesitant to participate in class activities were able to take on more prominent roles in the classroom as a result of taking on the role of podcaster).

Having decided on a focus for the show, the next step was to contact the children's parents/guardians to let them know about the project and to have them sign permission forms. With the consent of all the parents, the podcast project was quickly on its way. We also talked with the children about radio names or show names. Carol had a discussion with them about issues related to safety as the primary reason for taking on different roles and identities online. This helped the children to understand that anyone can assume a different identity online, which is why we always need to be careful of whom to trust and to be mindful of when we need to be cautious. The children were, therefore, not naïve to the existence of other people online that may not have their best interests in mind. Carol spoke with them about not blindly trusting people they met online, including those who may comment on their podcast. We did, however, take extra precautions and monitored the comments so that any inappropriate ones were deleted. In the case of *100% Kids*, other than some spam e-mail, all of the comments were appropriate.

The act of choosing radio names was very exciting as children were quick to realize that taking on these new names meant the ability to also construct new identities. Gee (2004, 2005) talks about new technology, like podcasting, as opening up possibilities for new forms of interacting that are quite motivating and compelling. For some, the act of renaming themselves into an alternate existence was transformative, and once shy and hesitant children for whom the curriculum was difficult to access were taking on new roles in the classroom. This fits Nixon and Gutiérrez's (2008) notion of identity play whereby children are able to extend the ways in which they are able to express themselves and tell their stories. As they play with language for publication in the online space, they develop an authorial stance or point of view from which they communicate their ideas. In doing so, they develop new identities as meaning makers (Nixon & Gutiérrez, 2008).

Maria, a shy, withdrawn 7-year-old identified with multiple learning issues, was one such child. When I first met her, she deliberately shied away from me and in fact she was rarely ever in the classroom when I was there. She barely spoke and did not have much to do with the other children, including their podcasting. In her journal, Carol wrote,

> Maria developed many difficulties with learning, speech, and hearing. She came to my class with an IEP [Individual Education Plan] for social skills and speech and language, which barely touched on how much more there was to learn about her struggles with learning. She mostly liked to be alone and work alone which stood out to me. I also could not understand what she said and this dilemma was true for many of the students in the class as well. There were many abrupt "what?!" from her classmates when we introduced ourselves in the first days [of school]. She tried hard, but much of what came out of her was not understandable. The kids wanted to know about her favorite foods and colors, so their questioning was in her best interests, but still hurt Maria because she was trying so hard to make herself understood.
>
> While Maria's classmates could not understand her, she could not always understand them either. She has partial hearing loss and uses an amplifying unit so that she can better hear and understand what someone is saying in whole-group sessions. I wore a microphone on days when I knew I could not speak as loud as I could. Maria had a seat on the rug next to me if we were in a circle or if we were in a group lesson, she had a place in the front. Still, I watched Maria just escape into her own world as lessons went too fast or if she was tired from the night before or from the amount of focus she needed to keep in order to comprehend what was going on. Maria had plenty of struggles to manage throughout the year.

I spent one to two mornings a week in the classroom during the fall 2006 and spring 2007. Maria would sit or stand along the periphery of the classroom. Slowly, she began watching what her classmates were doing and she started to listen in on some of their conversation. Eventually she listened, with the other children, to one of their shows. After having heard a couple of shows she became more and more interested and gave herself a radio name. She wanted to be known as Queen, a nickname her mom called her. This was a name that apparently made her feel good, safe, and wanted.

Prior to our first recording session, I talked with Queen about the equipment I was using and reassured her that we could record as many times as she wanted. My first recording session with Queen lasted about 15 minutes. Queen's debut performance consisted of one line, "We hope you like our painting of the world," which would be part of the art section of the podcast where there was a brief discussion regarding the piece of art used in the show notes.

It took six or seven takes and approximately 25 minutes of editing to produce what amounted to Queen's 2.5 seconds of audio. If this were another task she would have given up on it or not participated at all, but Queen hung in there. I had explained to her that we could cut out the pieces she wasn't happy with and leave in the pieces she liked. Knowing these editing tools were available, according to Gee (2003), lowered the consequences of failure and created a space for her to take on this new challenge.

Several shows later a different Queen emerged as she physically and emotionally moved from the periphery of the classroom to the center where classmates were. No longer was she recording with me as an individual child, she was now recording and engaging in banter with a group of girls. In subsequent episodes, Maria can be heard singing songs that she helped create with her classmates and saying things like, "You go, girl," or "That's right, girl." In her identity as Queen, she was able to position herself as part of a group of classmates who by the end of the year had become her friends. No program of study or mandated curriculum could have helped her with this. For Queen, the experience of podcasting was as transformative for her as it was for other children in the class.

Part of organizing the show included deciding on what segments to include. The children wanted an introduction to prepare their audience for listening to the show. They also wanted to have an art piece to post on the podcast homepage. The art piece was to represent the salient issues from the show. When possible, they wanted to include a song or two in connection with the topics to be discussed. They also decided on including a news segment or current events segment, a dedication piece, and finally an acknowledgment section.

Putting Together a Show

Recognizing the cross-curricular work that was part of putting together a show helped Carol to not limit the amount of time spent on crafting the scripts. Some days she and her students worked for 30 minutes and other days they spent the whole morning researching, writing, and revising. This was possible because Carol recognized the ways in which the work they were doing with podcasting cut across different content areas (see Table 11.3 for examples). She was, therefore, not worried about not having time to cover other areas of the second-grade curriculum. Throughout the process, they used the library and online resources to research their topics or themes.

From Monday to Thursday the children generated ideas for the show, choosing themes or topics to address based on their interests and inquiry questions. Some of these ideas were generated through their conversations and experiences outside of school, while other ideas were generated as they worked with various multimedia texts, including children's books. The children would write, revise, perform, and then revise again their various scripts until they had crafted a text they felt was meaningful to share with an audience. To do this, they often asked for one another's opinions. They worked collaboratively in small groups, drawing on one anothers' knowledge of particular topics or events and researching particular bits of information. They shared ideas with one another and helped one another in many ways. The parents/guardians played a role by helping with translating some of the episodes to Spanish.

Based on their interests and desires, as the children moved to doing different parts of the show, they mentored and ushered one another along. In a way they were doing what Gee (2003) refers to as a debugging of their experiences, thereby learning from the experiences of others as they took on new roles or exchanged roles in the production of the show. Knowledge was shared and distributed among the children, and groups were often cross-functional. What this meant was that children did not always stick to working with the same group of classmates; they had no problems with creating and re-creating new groups, depending on which part of the show they were interested in developing. Children like Maria, who at the start of the year had difficulty accessing learning, were able to take on different identities in the podcasting world that created space for them to participate in ways they hadn't previously.

TABLE 11.3

How the Podcast Work Cut Across Different Content Areas

Content Area	Standards of Learning	Literacies Produced Through Podcasting Work
Oral language, reading, and writing	2.3. The student will use oral communication skills. 2.9. The student will demonstrate comprehension of information in reference materials. 2.11. The student will write stories, letters, and simple explanations.	Producing a show involved: • Researching topics • Writing scripts: narrative, reports, jokes, songs, introductions, dedications, acknowledgments • Rehearsing scripts • Performing on the show • Taking on different identities • Critiquing and evaluating their performances • Reading and responding to comments
Science	2.4. The student will investigate and understand that plants and animals undergo a series of orderly changes in their life cycles. 2.5. The student will investigate and understand that living things are part of a system.	Science-based topics explored include: • Global warming • Endangered species • Sea and ocean life • Other environmental issues
Math	2.18 The student will use calendar language appropriately (e.g., months, today, yesterday, next week, last week); determine past and future days of the week; and identify specific dates on a given calendar.	Producing a show involved: • Creating timelines and schedules • Meeting deadlines • Prioritizing and ordering elements of the show • Deciding on possible topics to discuss on particular dates • Timing show episodes and scripts.
Social Studies	2.10c. The student will explain the responsibilities of a good citizen, with emphasis on describing actions that can improve the school and community.	The focus of the show was creating space to contribute to positive change in the community and beyond.

Putting together a show wasn't always easy. To attempt to put out a weekly show is quite an undertaking, but the children took on this challenge with excitement and without hesitation. This included researching their topics using both fiction and nonfiction books and electronic resources. This is consistent with two of Gee's (2003) principles of learning: Committed Learning Principle and Practice Principle. The first deals with learners participating in extended engagements, while the second deals with the ongoing rehearsing and rewriting of scripts where the repetitive nature of taking on each step of producing the show, week after week, never seemed to become boring for the child.

On Fridays, we would record the show one segment at a time. The children were quick to learn that using a digital recorder meant we could do as many takes as needed and that we could edit out extraneous artifacts and misreadings. Ben stated, "I would be surprised if in this day and age with what we can do with technology if we couldn't do that kind of editing." After recording the show, I edited the pieces together over the weekend and then released the show on the following Monday. (See Figure 11.3 for show notes. To listen to the show, go to www.bazmakaz.com/100kids.) Mondays were not only spent listening to the show as a group but also critiquing the audio (see Figure 11.4 for a student's critique of the show)

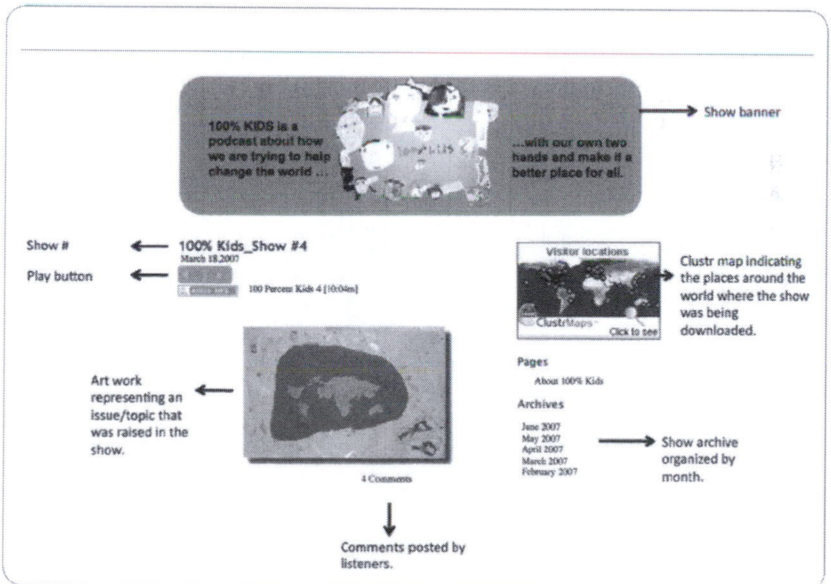

FIG. 11.3 Show Notes

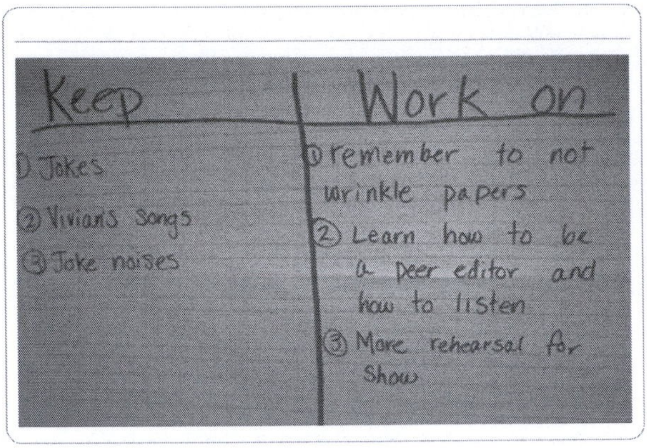

FIG. 11.4 Critique of the Show

and making adjustments to the upcoming episodes. In Figure 11.4, the column on the left represents the segments of the show that the children think should be continued or elements that should be added. The column on the right represents things the children feel they need to work on in order to produce a quality show.

It was during their critique of the show that the children came up with the idea of incorporating a jokes segment to give their audience a break from having to listen to the important issues and topics discussed in other segments of the show. They introduced this segment in Show #2.

Liam: Hi, my name is Drake. We are here to introduce a new part of the show called Jokey, Joke, Jokes.
Edwin C: We think this is important to make you laugh and give you a break from listening to all this hard work.
Edwin G: The jokes give us a break from all the hard work too!
Liam: Here we go! I hope your stomach doesn't hurt too much from laughing!

We Did It and So Can You!

The title of this section refers to Show #8, in which the children reported on a yearlong project they took on to enable the second graders in the school to go on a trip to the Baltimore Aquarium, after the school administration had decided the trip was too costly. Coming to second grade, the children had anticipated this year-end trip. The trip was especially important for some of the kids who, because of financial constraints in their homes, were counting on this trip as their only opportunity to go to the aquarium. Being told this tradition was no longer to be continued was very problematic, and it resulted in Carol's students taking social action to reverse this decision by organizing a series of fund-raising events. Their work involved using the Internet to research what they could learn from going to the aquarium, figuring out costs for the trip including entrance fees and transportation and so forth. They also met with the principal on two occasions to discuss their displeasure at having the trip cancelled and to lay out a plan of action. They engaged in multiple activities to make the trip happen. They talked about their work, sharing sentiments of amazement and joy, in their show.

> Kia: Hi, I'm Kia. We went to the Baltimore Aquarium. That's what we did on May 8, Tuesday. Our class finally got the whole second grade to go to the Baltimore Aquarium. I think it's amazing how a bunch of second graders got all the second graders in our school to go to the Baltimore Aquarium. It's all so wonderful. Bye.

Figure 11.5 is the post for Show #8. It includes letters written to Carol's class thanking them for all their hard work in succeeding to

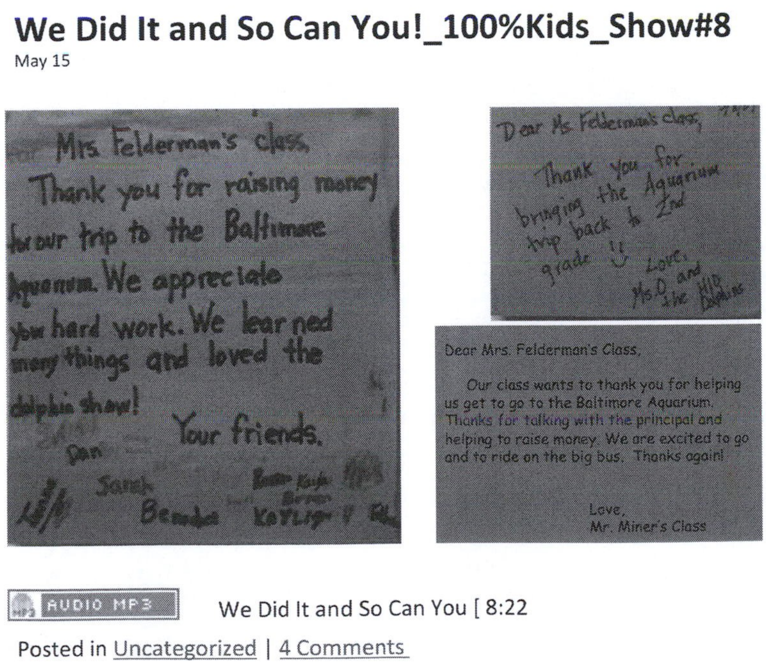

FIG. 11.5 Show #8 (We Did It and So Can You!) Post

send the second graders on a trip to the Baltimore Aquarium. Also included were comments from listeners congratulating the children on their accomplishment.

Connecting Across Time and Place

I was with the children as they listened to their final show of the year. The celebration included both family and friends. One of the mothers approached me, asking,

> Parent: Are you Vivian?
> Me: Yes, I am.
> Parent: I have to say thank you for doing this [podcasting] with the kids.

With tears in her eyes, she continued, "My family doesn't live together because we cannot. Her father, he lives in Columbia. He waits for this [podcast] each week so he can hear her [his daughter's voice]."

Apparently, the release of each episode was the highlight of the week for him. He listened to the show at an Internet café in Columbia along with other family members. The family had been divided and living in different countries as a way to create a better life for themselves. It was an extraordinary surprise to discover that the children's podcast had this kind of impact.

For the children, producing, designing, and redesigning episodes and segments included in their podcast created a space to get at the notion that texts are socially constructed and that literacy is most definitely not a neutral technology. Through the issues they researched and talked about on the show, as well as through their own experiences in learning about how they each could contribute to this shared experience, they learned about ways they are positioned within certain social systems and the discursive practices or ways of being, doing, speaking, and acting that shape these and the ways in which they position others through the choices they make. They learned to use what the technology afforded them to reach and connect with people beyond the physical limitations of their school site. Connecting with people in other spaces and places allows children to hear the perspective of others and helps them make more informed decisions as participants of the world around them.

The use of new technology made accessible to them knowledge that they could not have gained in a pre-technological age. For instance, while using the Internet, they learned about what other young people have done in other spaces and places, using social networking tools like podcasting.

Throughout this process, students drew from their cultural and semiotic resources, moved beyond more traditional ways of working with texts, including children's literature and creating texts, and in the end the experience was transformative for many of them. Podcasting and new technologies became tools used for thinking about the world and for learning and communicating—as well as representing some critical literacy work that takes into account the stuff of everyday life, everyday social issues and events, and children's existing literacy practices, and that creates opportunities for engaging in social action projects.

Reflection Questions

1. In what ways do you currently use technology in your setting? In what ways do your students currently use technology in their everyday lives? What kinds of resources, support, hardware, and software do you imagine you would need to explore the use of technology in your setting?
2. What might get in the way of your using technology? How might you get past this hurdle?
3. What sorts of technological tools are you interested in using? To do what kind of work and for what purpose?
4. In what ways are you interested in connecting with others via the Internet? For what reasons? For what purpose(s)?
5. What might you do differently with the use of technology? What might your students be able to do differently?

Try This

1. Take inventory of the technological tools you might have in your classroom. Then survey with what sorts of technology your students might be familiar. What are possible ways you might use the technology and technological resources you have available in the work that you and your students do in the classroom?

2. Listen to a few episodes of *100% Kids* Podcast. Discuss with your students how they might one day use technology in the way Carol's students did to make accessible to others what they were thinking and learning.
   - What topics or issues might you consider?
   - What segments might you include?
   - What show names might you choose?
   - What difference would this show you are considering make in the world? For whom would your show make a difference?

Resource Box 11.1 Texts That Focus on Critical Literacy and Technology

Comber, B., & Kamler B. (Eds). (2005). *Turn-around pedagogies*. Newtown, NSW: Primary English Teaching Association.
Comber, B., & Simpson, A. (Eds). (2001). *Negotiating critical literacies in classrooms*. Mahwah, NJ: Erlbaum.
Gee, J. P., & Hayes, E. R. (2011). *Language and learning in the digital age*. New York: Routledge.
Janks, H. (2010). *Literacy and power*. New York: Routledge.
Larson, J., & Marsh, J. (2005). *Making literacy real*. Thousand Oaks, CA: Sage.
Marsh, J. (2002). Popular culture, computer games and the primary curriculum. In M. Monteith, M. (Ed.), *Teaching primary literacy through ICT* (pp. 127–143). Buckinghamshire, UK: Open University Press.
Marsh, J. (Ed). (2005). *Popular culture, new media and digital literacy in early childhood*. New York: Routledge.
Marsh, J., et al. (2005). *Digital beginnings: Young People's use of popular culture, media and new technologies*. Sheffield, UK: University of Sheffield Research Center.
Vasquez, V. (2014). *Negotiating critical literacies with young children*. New York: Routledge.
Vasquez, V., & Felderman, C. (2013). *Technology and critical literacy in early childhood*. New York: Routledge.
Wohlwend, K. (2011). *Playing their way into literacies*. New York: Teachers College Press.

12

Negotiating Spaces for Critical Literacies in Health and Physical Education

The chart in Figure 12.1 is representative of a larger chart created by Christine Paul's third-grade students while engaged in an in-depth study of gender stereotypes at their school. Their school is the same one described earlier in chapter 11. In this chapter I venture into areas of the curriculum that are not often associated with critical literacies—namely, physical education and health. This chart, and the work of which it was a part, serves as a backdrop for Christine's students' engagement with critical literacies during physical education class.

Boys	Girls
Boys like blue. Boys are mean. Boys like bugs. Boys are stronger than girls. All boys like to read.	Girls like pink. Girls wear dresses. Girls don't like bugs. Girls slap and not punch. All girls like sports.

FIG. 12.1 Problematic Assumptions About Boys and Girls

Checking Gender at the Gymnasium Door

Christine: During physical education class one day, my students noticed that the girls played at lower basketball hoops than the boys.

As previously mentioned at the time of this observation, Christine and her students had been exploring gender stereotypes at their school. The chart at the start of this chapter is a micro version of a larger chart they had created to discuss various problematic assumptions about boys and girls that they observed at their school (see Figure 12.1). In response to findings such as what is posted on the chart, Christine and her students worked to find ways of responding to inequitable issues, such as gender stereotypes, they were seeing around them. Their responses to these issues took many forms, including writing petitions, creating public service announcements, creating documentaries, and making posters to circulate throughout their school. Each of these projects was done to make visible inequities and stereotypes as a way to disrupt them. This of course involved time spent getting to know various tools for communicating their concerns and considering what each would afford the work they were doing. For instance, what effect would watching a public service announcement have that might be different from reading or viewing a poster?

In response to the hoop issue, a small group of students decided to write three letters—one to the principal and one to each of the Physical Education teachers. In the letters, they articulated their concern with stereotyping girls by having them use the low hoops. In class they discussed the various assumptions that went with such stereotypes. Some of these were consistent with those posted on their assumptions chart. Christine did a series of short writing lessons with her students to support them as they drafted their letters. While considering what types of letters to write, the students learned about friendly correspondence, business letters, and persuasive writing. They also discussed what questions and topics they felt needed to be addressed in their letter, such as what school practices and procedures they wanted changed, why they thought change was needed, and how this change might take place. Before they wrote, Christine gave a lesson on respectful writing and language use. As her students drafted their letters, they simultaneously began to realize the power of words and thus the relationship between language and power. Together Christine and her students also deconstructed their own texts and debated their word choices as they wrote their letters and as they completed other projects.

Another text they created was a survey, which they circulated around the school to find out if a petition was warranted to change the stereotypic gendered practice in gym class. In their survey they wrote:

> Dear Teachers,
>
> We are getting kind of concerned with the low hoops and high hoops in P.E. We don't like that the girls get the little hoops and the boys get the big hoops. So we are going to make a petition about it. A petition is a type of social action. Will you give these words to your children and please do these directions?
>
> 1. Get your class together.
> 2. Tell them we've been doing a project on petitions and stereotypes.
> 3. Have students pick one column they agree with.
> 4. Tell sheet 2 to your class. (Explain the survey sheet to your class.)
> 5. If your class doesn't understand one word then please EXPLAIN!!!
> 6. Pass the petition around and have your kids sign it in the column they agree with.
> 7. Put finished petitions in Mrs. Paul's mailbox by June 7.

Column 1	Column 2	Column 3
We don't think it's fair that boys get the big hoops. We think the hoops should be equal height.	We don't think it's fair that boys get the big hoops. We think the hoops should be mixed.	We don't think it's fair that boys get the big hoops. We think the hoops should be switched every time.

In the words of Mem Fox, the children ached with caring over the work they accomplished. They did this because they knew the potential impact the work they were doing could have even if the initial reaction to their actions were challenged. They knew that calling attention to the issues brought those issue to fore and that as a result of their work, people in their community were now aware of those issues.

Christine: By playing with words (in their letter writing, while constructing their public service announcement script, and creating their documentary), my students became more aware of how other writers create texts and how they might be positioned as readers of these texts. They not only became critical readers, they also learned the power of being critical writers and responsible conduits for social action.

They did this with the use of multimodal tools. Excited about the literacies produced through their critical work, together with Suzanne Whaley, Christine reflected on the process she and her students went through as they carried out their critical work. Together, they referred to the process as a critical inquiry cycle (Figure 12.2), which became, for Christine, an important framework for creating

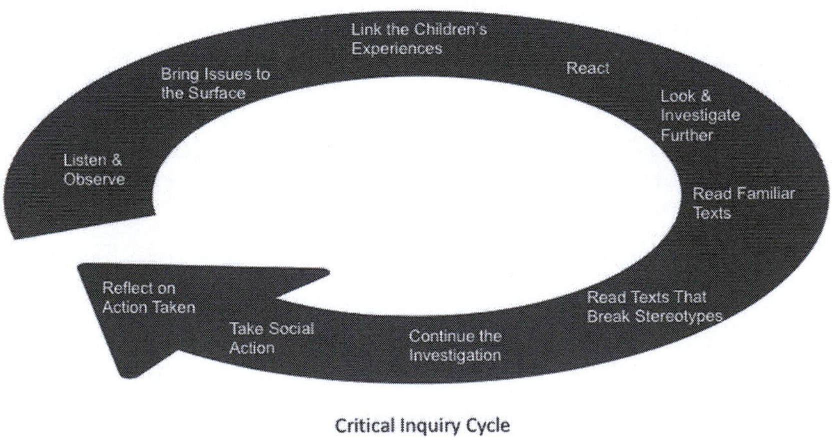

FIG. 12.2A Critical Inquiry Cycle and Critical Inquiry Cycle in Action

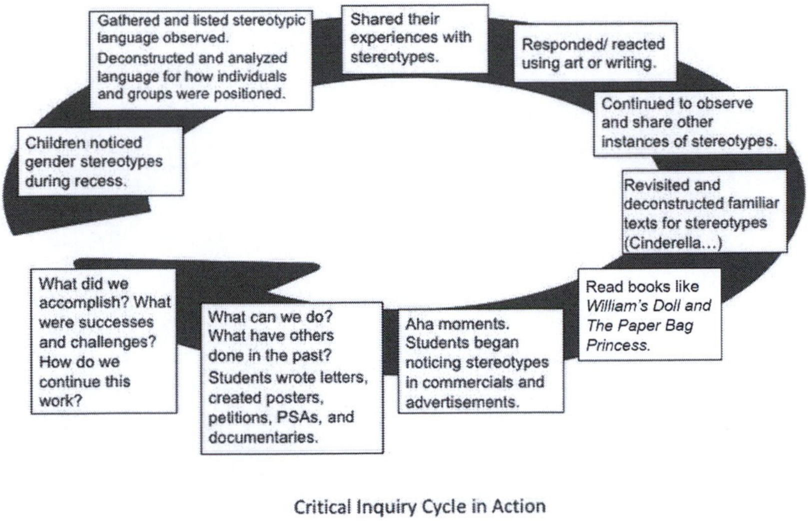

FIG. 12.2B

spaces for critical literacies in her classroom. (See Figure 12.2 for the cycle in action during the work on gender stereotypes.)

Critical Literacy and Health Education

Unpacking Fruity Peel-Outs

The image in Figure 12.3 is a re-design of the front matter for the packaging of a snack food popular with young children created by 5-year-old Emily. She was part of a group of five 3- to 5-year-old pre-school students with whom I spent time exploring the use of everyday public and social texts as sites for taking up social issues from a critical literacy perspective.

There were two girls and three boys in the group. The pre-school was located in a highly multicultural, middle to low-income community in a suburb of Toronto, Ontario, Canada. Many of the children at the school received government subsidies. Having worked as a consultant in the school, I was given permission to work independently with the group of five children. The focus of our work was on analyzing everyday text as one way to make visible the power of taking up such texts as tools for understanding how language works and the

FIG. 12.3 "People like to be happy and this is happy." Emily, 5 years old

importance of practicing the use of language in powerful ways to get things done in the world (Comber, 2001a).

Including my work with these children in this chapter on physical education and health was deliberate. That our work highlights health and nutrition issues was a matter of happenstance. For the most part, my attempts at creating spaces for critical literacies are not a matter of putting the content area or subject matter first. What is at center are things of importance to the children: their issues, questions, inquiries and wonderings. From that center, ways of exploring those things of importance are generated with the use of multimodal texts, tools, and resources. So I generally do not start by creating space to do some critical science or critical math work with children. Rather, I begin with what's important to them and then create spaces for exploring that topic using different critical lenses: What might this look from a critical literacy perspective through the eyes of a mathematician or scientist? As mentioned previously, I have long believed that a critical literacy curriculum needs to he lived and that as teachers we need to incorporate a critical perspective into our everyday lives with our students in order to find ways to help children understand the social and political issues around them. Given this belief it makes perfect sense to use texts of everyday life as objects of study and simultaneously explore intersections within different areas of the curriculum.

A Look at Early Critical Literacy Practices Using Snack Packages

The work described in this section of the chapter deals with the deconstruction and re-design of a Fruity Peel-Outs box. Fruity Peel-Outs are candy fruit snacks for children. Sheets of sweet, sticky, pliable candy come rolled up in individual packages ready for children's consumption. On the first day of the study, one of the preschoolers happened to bring a box of these candies to school.

The Fruity Peel-Outs box generated immediate interest to others in the group as they began calling out things they noticed on it. Capitalizing on this interest and recalling the work done by Comber and Simpson (1995) on analyzing cereal boxes, I asked them to pass the box around and had each child name one thing on it that they noticed. While they did this, I kept a list of all the items they mentioned. Andre started. "I spy with my little eye Mickey Mouse!" Rola followed, "I spy with my little eye some fruit!" They continued in this fashion, integrating one of their favorite games, "I Spy," into the textual analysis we were attempting. For me this was a reminder of possibilities for the ongoing creation of curricular spaces for critical literacy as we moved back and forth between my capitalizing on their interests in the popular snack and their capitalizing on the activity I had initiated by integrating, into the naming activity, the game "I Spy."

What is difficult in creating these curricular spaces is resisting over-schooling the children's topics and co-opting their interests, thereby diminishing their pleasure with them. These spaces therefore need to be negotiated carefully with respectful attention paid to the interests of the children.

We continued our activity by talking about what kind of work each piece of information could accomplish and discussing who might want that information and why. Part of our conversation included the ways in which words and images work together and apart to produce different effects for the reader. Emily theorized that children would be interested in the cartoon images on the box. She noted, "I want the information about peeling the Mickey Mouse shape." She continued by saying she liked the Peel-Outs better than other snacks because of the Mickey Mouse shapes in the fruity candy. She was clear on the fact that what drew her to the snack was the image of Mickey Mouse. The group agreed that other children would likely be enticed by the cartoon images as well. For Emily the 'fruitiness' of the candy was secondary, if it had any importance at all.

Miguel, on the other hand, suggested that his father would want the fruit (pointing at the image of an apple, peach, and berry on the box), not necessarily the fruity candy, because "that's yucky good for you." Apparently his father only lets him eat 'good' snacks. Although he agreed that such foods were good for his health, Miguel sometimes felt they were yucky. What is notable here is the distinction made between something 'fruity,' which is not as healthy as an actual 'fruit.' Without too much discussion, the children quickly picked up on the use of the adjective 'fruity' as a way to make the snack seem healthier and that this, in combination with images of fruit, intensified the extent to which the snack was portrayed as healthy. As such through discussion the children were learning more and more not only about the power of language but also about semantics and syntax.

Once we had established that various texts and images are desirable to different groups of people and for different reasons, we continued by talking about how, in particular, the words and images work. We began to unpack the linguistic features on the box, analyzing the effects, on the reader, of the words, pictures, and symbols. I did this with them as one way to begin identifying the cultural values being promoted and presented, for whom, and in what ways. For instance, in a society that is bombarded with informational text on the nutritional values of food, it is no wonder that Miguel raised the health aspect issue of the Peel-Outs.

To take our work deeper, I discussed with the children what they thought were good ideas and bad ideas for texts and images to be included on the box if they were to be re-designed. Following were some of their responses.

Andrei

Andrei thought it would be a good idea to include images of fruit and kids to show that the fruits are good for the kids. He thought it was a bad idea to have anything having to do with dirt or garbage because that isn't good for kids.

(See Figure 12.4B — Andrei).

Geoffrey

Geoffrey also thought it would be a good idea to include fruit. He likes the Peel-Outs and said his mom would buy them if they were good for him, "and if there's fruit in them she'll buy them." He thought it would be a bad idea to have a person's name like "Geoffrey" because then "other kids who aren't Geoffrey won't think they should buy it."

(See Figure 12.4C — Geoffrey).

FIG. 12.4A The Children's 'Ideas' by Miguel

FIG. 12.4B by Andrei

FIG. 12.4C by Geoffrey

Emily

Emily drew her family to represent something good that would make them buy the Peel-Outs. She said "people like to be happy and this is happy" (See Figure 12.3). Note that Emily puts on offer a lifestyle as a conceptual frame for selling fruity Peel-Outs. She referred to her design as "the same as on T.V.," referring to recent ads for such companies as Target, Gap, and Old Navy that portray family and peer activities and people doing enjoyable things together as a concept for selling clothing, using very subtle branding of these products. So clearly, different communicative processes are thrown in the mix.

Miguel

Miguel drew a picture of bees to represent a bad idea, stating, "If you are allergic then aha—you'll be scared to death to buy this" (See Figure 12.4A — Miguel). He also puts on offer a particular lifestyle that promotes well-being and safety.

Hilary Janks (1993a) notes that identifying discourses that are at work in texts is an important part of reading critically and interrogating texts. Already, the children, through their selections of good and bad ideas, are making visible the discursive life styles (namely, health, safety, and happiness) or ways of being that would lead someone—in particular, adults in their lives—to buy or not buy the Peel-Outs.

Following this we talked about how language works on consumers, such as themselves. We discussed how words, images, and symbols on the food packaging work to position the 'buyer' of the product as a believer, someone who puts faith in what the product claims to deliver. In doing so we touched on the feelings and emotions that are encouraged and promoted through combinations of words and images. We also discussed the notion of temptation and how consumers might be tempted to buy particular products or goods, and the role that different elements, such as font style or color, might play.

Having done some deconstructive work, we turned our attention to re-designing and creating our own versions of the Peel-Out boxes. To do this I gave the children the option of using a black line to represent the front section of the box (See Figure 12.5).

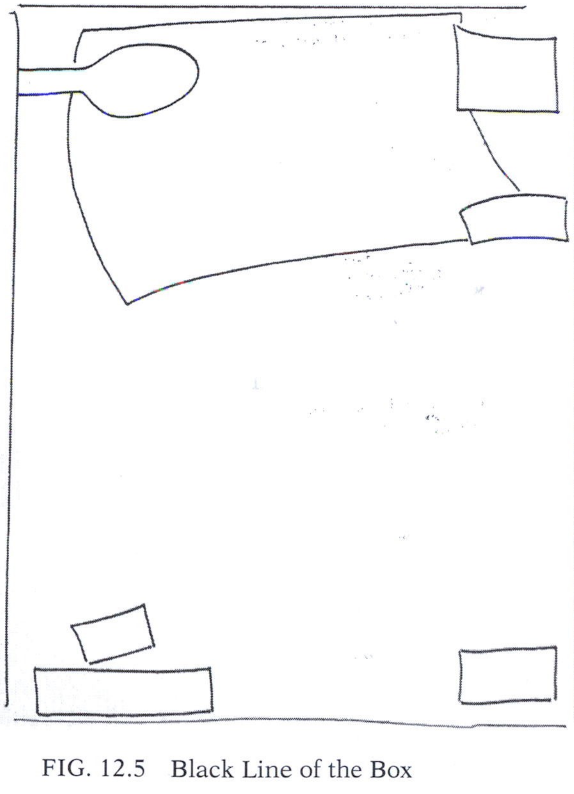

FIG. 12.5 Black Line of the Box

The children then took their collection of good ideas and used them to re-design the Peel-Out box. Following this they considered whether words would or would not help sell the product. Emily felt that words would not be helpful if they were on the box, but words would be helpful in a television commercial. Without hesitation, the children stood from their chairs and began acting out their good ideas.

We talked about who would say which lines and where they would position themselves in the shot. Miguel held up a make-believe camera in what became his directorial debut. "And . . . action," he called out, signaling for the performance to begin. With this Emily entered stage left, humming all the while. "Cut . . . cut!" the director called out. "Just walk the dog, don't hum!" he said firmly. If you recall, a dog was part of Emily's concept for the commercial. Nowhere in her drawing had she hinted at music as an integral part of her 'good idea.' Nevertheless, we talked about the potential use of music and what kind of music would work or not work, discussing how loud or how soft it should be and why, along with what effects different kinds of music would have on the viewer. More and more, learning was generated as we further deconstructed the Fruity Peel-Outs box, looking at other areas of the curriculum and talking in the language of science or math from a critical literacy perspective.

We also went online to take a look at the website of the company that manufactures the Fruity Peel-Outs. While on the site, we discovered a comments page. Deciding on whether or not to submit a comment resulted in another flurry of discussion and activity in which the children debated over what to say in their comment. During this debate we talked about how the size of the comment box limits what you can say in terms of the number of words you can use as well as the communication system through which to convey your message. We talked about possible reasons for the limited space for comment and came up with a short list, including "maybe the company wants to hear a little from us, but not a lot" and "maybe they don't really want to hear from us but maybe they just think they have to say they want to know what we think." When we didn't hear back after submitting our comments and suggestions, the children returned to their thoughts regarding the comment box and discussed further whether companies really do pay lip service to thoughts from consumers and talked about other possible ways that consumers could get their comments across to such companies as the manufacturer of the Fruity Peel-Outs.

When I first decided to capitalize on the children's interest in the food packaging, I had not anticipated or imagined the learning and literacies that might emerge. I am certain, however, that the learning that unfolded may not have unfolded as it did if we had been working from a limited, bound, mandated prescriptive curriculum. Imagine how much more accessible a curriculum that incorporates the use of everyday text and print would be for a linguistically and culturally diverse group of learners. One of the advantages of using popular culture and everyday print is that the texts used can and should be negotiated with the children based on what is interesting and intriguing to them and using textual materials available in their lives.

Becoming Informed by Children's Unexpected and Problematic Performances

Comber and Simpson (1995) note that we need to be informed by children's unexpected responses and problematic performances to see what kinds of readers, writers, spellers, speakers, listeners, and viewers they are becoming. Often these unexpected responses come from the everyday issues they bring with them to the classroom. The problematic comes into play as we define these issues as extra-curricular, distractive, or disconnected from school literacy. So how do we capitalize on children's unexpected and problematic performances? A place to start is by carving out spaces in the curriculum for practicing critical literacies and putting into effective use the issues that children raise, using language to:

- question
- interrogate
- problematize
- de-naturalize
- interrupt
- disrupt

that which appears

- normal
- natural
- ordinary

- mundane
- everyday

as well as to

- re-design
- re-construct
- re-imagine
- re-think
- re-consider

social worlds, spaces, and places.

In this chapter I highlighted work done in a physical education setting and work done to explore issues such as health and nutrition with young learners. In reality this chapter could have focused on math or science, depending on how I might have chosen to frame the telling of the experiences shared. With the pre-school children, I attempted to provide opportunities to examine the ideologies of everyday texts that they brought to the classroom to provide opportunities for them to begin practicing critical literacies while also learning to negotiate meaning, participating as code breakers, text participants, text users and critical analysts of everyday, social and school texts (Luke & Freebody, 1999b). Christine did the same with her third-grade students. There is much we can learn from these new textual practices. What I have shared in this chapter is a mere snippet of possibility.

Reflection Questions

When you think about creating spaces for critical literacy, what kinds of topics, issues, or texts come to mind? What areas of the curriculum might be encompassed by those topics, issues, or texts? What areas of the curriculum have not made it on your list? Were physical education or health education on your list? If not, how might you frame one of the topics or issues you have identified from a physical education or health education perspective?

Try This

- For an entire school day, list all of the everyday texts that your students interact with in some way or talk about in some way. Make sure to add everyday texts that they come into contact with even if they do not talk about those texts in any way.

- At the end of the day, have a look through your list and think about the topics or issues that could be addressed using each of the texts.
- Think about what multimodal texts, from different content areas, you might pair with each text to explore particular topics or issues further. Make sure to also consider framing your work from a critical health education perspective and/or a critical physical education perspective.

13

Doing "Important Work"

Teacher:	I can't believe that it's already June.
Patricia:	Yeah. September, October, November . . . June.
Alexandro:	Lots of months, lots of learning.
Emma:	And lots of books. I like books.
Alexandro:	Yes . . . books and more books.
Teacher:	What are some things you've learned about books this year?
Alexandro:	When we talked about books, mostly we talked about us.
Teacher:	Tell me more about that.
Emma:	Not just words, right?
Patricia:	Right. Mostly our talk and using words and pictures to do important work like changing what's not fair.
Alexandro:	Sometimes that's hard, but sometimes not so hard.
Patricia:	But that's important work, right, Emma?
Emma:	Right, Patricia.

It was the end of the school year. My kindergarten students, whom you met at the beginning of this book, sat informally chatting about the year that had passed. Their talk focused on their work with books and how that work was sometimes hard and sometimes not so hard, but most importantly, they understood they had done important work to contribute to changing "what's not fair."

The "important work" that Patricia and Emma referred to in this exchange includes the experiences we had with all sorts of multimodal texts—using texts not just for pleasure or enjoyment but also for creating spaces to understand how language works to construct people, for using language to critique the word and the world, and for changing social practices that give an advantage to some people over others. Putting in place a critical literacy framework made it possible for my students and me to investigate the positions taken up by texts, so that I was able to help my students become literate beings who question things that are taken for granted or are assumed to be normal or natural in the world. My students and I did this by critically reading with and against diverse multimodal texts in different content or subject areas of the curriculum, thereby analyzing the world in which we live. We analyzed the things with which we agreed and disagreed, and we imagined new or revised versions of those things. All the other teachers whose classrooms we visited worked to do the same.

Not Just Words

If you recall, I opened this book with a conversation between Patricia and Alexandro regarding their disappointment in discovering that there were no books about the Philippines in our school library even though there were large numbers of Filipino students in our school. Their concern was mainly for their new classmate, Emma, who had just arrived from the Philippines. Therefore, it is ironic to notice that in the previous conversation it was Emma who noted that books are "not just words, right?"

The teachers whose classrooms you visited in this book share Emma's sentiments that books and other multimodal texts that are part of our everyday lives are "not just words." In each of their classrooms, they used books and other texts as tools across the curriculum for learning language and learning about language, for using language to critique, and in so doing, to question, interrogate, problematize, denaturalize, interrupt, and disrupt that which appears normal and natural with an eye for redesigning or reimagining the social worlds, spaces, and places in which we live. Using language to critique helped each of us to understand that all texts are ideological sites or spaces for systemic values to reside. This includes the ever-increasing number of multimedia images that we come across in a given day.

It has been over 20 years since I began exploring what critical literacy could mean in different settings (Vasquez, 1994). In particular my work has focused on young children primarily between age 3 and 8 (Vasquez, 2000a, 2000b, 2001a, 2001b, 2001c, 2003a, 2003b). Of the work I have done, especially with pre-school aged children, a consistent question asked of me has been, "Do young kids really talk about social issues or equity issues?" and "Why can't we just let them be kids?" This is often followed with "Preschoolers don't really talk like that, do they?" (meaning as critical participants and analysts). My experience in working with young children has proven time and time again that children are in fact very capable and willing to participate in hard conversations that are meaningful to them and that impact their lives. Sometimes it is adults that have difficulty with this, often due to a feeling of uncertainty regarding how to talk about difficult topics or issues with children. When this happens, the literacies with which they can participate in the world are 'bound' (Rowe, 2005) since children are only able to speak using the discourses that have been made available to them or for which they have had access. This implies that part of schooling therefore needs to be about making accessible dominant and powerful discursive practices that create spaces for young learners to participate differently in the world.

It is a hard time to be a child these days. Day in and day out children take in multimodal bits of information consisting of words and images that sometimes conflict and at other times are complementary. Often this textual information works to position them in ways that offer up ideals for who they can and cannot be in the world today, who they should and should not be, as well as what they should and should not do or think. Given this complex world, we cannot afford for children not to engage in some tough conversations if they are to learn to become critical analysts of the world who are able to make informed decisions as they engage with the world around them.

Often issues of social justice and equity seem to be looked upon as heavy-handed issues. However, the discussions I have had with my students and the children who have participated in my research tell me otherwise. The actions we took and the work we accomplished, although often serious, were very pleasurable. We enjoyed our work because the topics that we dealt with were socially significant to us in the same way that the topics and issues explored in the K–6 classrooms highlighted in this book were of importance to the children in those classrooms.

The teachers whose stories were shared and I were at different places in our conceptualization of critical literacy as I created this book. Given a different time and space, different stories may have been told, and different texts may have been used to practice the use of language in more powerful ways. One common denominator in each of our stories, however, is that all of us attempted to create spaces in our particular locations to engage in the "important work" referred to by Patricia and Emma. I hope that this book helps you to do the same.

Reflection Questions

1. Now that you have had a chance to read about possibilities for working across the curriculum from a critical literacy perspective, what are some possibilities that you have imagined for engaging with critical literacies across the curriculum in your setting?
2. What can you imagine to be possible road-blocks and how might you get beyond such barriers? What resources or support would be helpful for you?
3. How might you make accessible to others the work that you do so that they may learn from your experience?

Resource Box 13.1 Resources on Critical Literacy in Practice

Comber, B., & Simpson, A. (Eds.). (2001). *Negotiating critical literacies in classrooms*. Mahwah, NJ: Erlbaum.

Comber, B., & Thomson, P. (with Wells, M.). (2001). Critical literacy finds a "place": Writing and social action in a low-income Australian grade 2/3 classroom. *The Elementary School Journal,* 101(4), 451–464.

Edelsky, C. (Ed.). (2000). *Making justice our project: Teachers working toward critical whole language practice*. Urbana, IL: National Council of Teachers of English.

Fehring, H., & Green, P. (Eds.). (2001). *Critical literacy: A collection of articles from the Australian Literacy Educators' Association*. Newark, DE: International Reading Association.

Heffernan, L., & Lewison, M. (2000). Making real-world issues our business: Critical literacy in a third-grade classroom. *Primary Voices K–6*, 9(2), 15–21.

Janks, H. (2014). *Doing critical literacy*. New York: Routledge.

Janks, H., & Comber, B. (2005). Critical literacy across continents. In J. Larson & J. Marsh (2005). *Making literacy real: Theories and practices for learning and teaching*. Thousand Oaks, CA: Sage.

Luke, A. (2007). The new literacies. *Webcasts and podcasts for educators*. Retrieved from www.curriculum.org/secretariat/may31.shtml

Marsh, J. (2000). "But I want to fly too!": Girls and superhero play in the infant classroom. *Gender and Education*, 12(2), 209–220.

Mellor, B., O'Neill, M., & Patterson, A. (2000). *Reading stories: Activities and texts for critical readings*. Urbana, IL: National Council of Teachers of English.

Morgan, W. (1997). *Critical literacy in the classroom: The art of the possible*. New York: Routledge.

Muspratt, S., Luke, A., & Freebody, P. (1997). *Constructing critical literacies: Teaching and learning textual practice*. Cresskill, NJ: Hampton.

O'Brien, J. (1994). Show Mum you love her: Taking a new look at junk mail. *Reading*, 28(1), 43–46.

Vasquez, V. (1998). Building equitable communities: Taking social action in a kindergarten classroom. *Talking Points*, 9(2), 3–6.

Vasquez, V. (2000). Building community through social action. *School Talk*, 5(4), 2–3.

Vasquez, V. (2000). Language stories and critical literacy lessons. *Talking Points*, 11(2), 5–7.

Vasquez, V. (2013). *Technology and critical literacy in early childhood*. New York: Routledge.

Vasquez, V. (2014). *Negotiating critical literacies with young children*. Mahwah, NJ: Erlbaum.

Resource Box 13.2 Critical Literacy: Influences Over Time

This resource box offers a glimpse into theoretical orientations and influences through the years that have helped shape what we know as critical literacy.

1920s Frankfurt School

- Focus on Critical Theory.
- Created by intellectuals who carved out a space for developing theories of Marxism within the academy and independently of political parties.
- Emphasized the importance of class struggle in society.

1940s Paulo Freire

- Focused on critical consciousness and critical pedagogy.
- Work centered on key concepts, which included the notion that literacy education should highlight the critical consciousness of learners.

1987 Macedo and Freire

- Brought forth the notion that when we read the word we simultaneously read the world.

1960s Paulo Freire

- Organized a campaign for hundreds of sugar cane workers in Brazil to participate in a literacy program that centered on critical pedagogy.
- Became known for liberatory work through which he worked to empower oppressed workers.
- Critiques of Freire have focused primarily on claims that the liberatory pedagogy he espoused was unidirectional because educators liberated students.

1996 New London Group

- Group of ten academics, including James Gee and Allan Luke.

- Concerned about how literacy pedagogy might address the rapid change in literacy due to globalization, technology, and increasing cultural and social diversity.
- Developed pedagogy of multiliteracies.

1999 Freebody and Luke: Four Resources Model

- Widely adapted for use in classrooms from pre-school to tertiary education settings.
- Model focuses on different literacy practices that readers and writers should learn.
- These practices are learning to be code breakers—recognizing, understanding, and using the fundamental features of written text, such as the alphabet; learning to be text participants—using their own prior knowledge to interpret and make meaning from text; understanding how to use different text forms; and becoming critical consumers of those forms—learning to critically analyze text and understanding that texts are never neutral.

Early 2000s Green's 3D Model of Literacy

- Multidimensional framework that argues that there are always three dimensions of literacy simultaneously at play: the operational, learning how the language works and ways that texts can be structured; the cultural, which involves the uses of literacy and in particular the ways that cultural learning is involved with content learning; and the critical, the ways in which we act and see in the world along with how literacy can be used to shape lives in ways that better serve the interests of some over others.
- Useful frame for unpacking links between literacy, place, and culture.

2000 Janks

- Developed an interdependent framework for critical literacy.
- Framework includes four dimensions: power, diversity, access, and design/redesign.

- Focusing on any one of these dimensions without any one of the other dimensions is insufficient.
- Framework was distilled from a careful reading of the literature in a range of education-related areas—anti-racism, whiteness, feminism, post-colonialism, sexual orientation, critical linguistics, critical pedagogy, socio-cultural and critical approaches to literacy, and critical discourse analysis.

2016 Comber

- Spatiality and place-based pedagogies.
- Incorporates complex understandings of the cultural and political histories, and the dynamic potential, of the places in which school communities are located.
- Teachers work with children as co-researchers through the study of people's lives in particular places and times.
- Study of complex histories become a powerful resource for building young people's literacy repertoires.

Resource Box 13.3 Influential Theoretical Orientations

Various theoretical paradigms and traditions of scholarship have influenced definitions of critical literacy, how it is circulated, as well as how it is practiced. Those include the following:

- Feminist post-structuralist theories (Davies, 1993; Gilbert, 1992)
- Post-colonialist traditions (Meacham, 2003)
- Critical race theory (Ladson-Billings, 1999, 2003)
- Critical linguistics and critical discourse analysis (Fairclough, 1995, Janks, 2010)
- Cultural studies (Pahl & Rowsell, 2011)
- Critical media literacy (Share, 2009, 2010)
- Queer theory (Vicars, 2013)
- Place-conscious pedagogy (Comber, 2016).

Resource Box 13.4 New Directions in the Field of Critical Literacy

New directions in the field of critical literacy reiterate and remind us of what educators working in the field of critical literacy have maintained (Comber, 2016; Janks, 2014; Luke, 2014; Vasquez, 2014b)—that there is no correct or universal model of critical literacy. This means "how educators deploy the tools, attitudes, and philosophies is utterly contingent . . . upon students' and teachers' everyday relations of power, their lived problems and struggles" (Luke, 2014, p. 29) and the ways in which teachers are able to navigate the (P)politics of the places and spaces in which their work unfolds.

New directions in the field of critical literacy include:

- Finding new ways to engage with multimodalities and new technologies (Comber, 2016; Janks & Vasquez, 2011; Larson & Marsh, 2015; Nixon, 2003; Nixon & Comber, 2005)
- Engaging with spatiality and place-based pedagogies (Comber, 2016; Comber & Nixon, 2014)
- Working across the curriculum in the content areas (Comber & Nixon, 2014; Janks, 2014; Vasquez, 2017).

Further Reading

Comber, B. (2013). Critical literacy in the early years: Emergence and sustenance in an age of accountability. In J. Larson & J. Marsh (Eds.), *The SAGE handbook of early childhood literacy* (pp. 587–601). London: SAGE.

Comber, B. (2016). *Literacy, place, and pedagogies of possibility*. New York: Routledge.

Janks, H. (2010). *Literacy and power*. New York & London: Routledge.

Kamler, B. (2001). *Relocating the personal: A critical writing pedagogy*. New York: State University of New York Press.

Lewison, M., Leland, C., & Harste, J. C. (2014). *Creating critical classrooms: Reading and writing with an edge* (2nd ed.). New York: Routledge.

Luke, A. (2013). Regrounding critical literacy: Representation, facts and reality. In M. Hawkins (Ed.), *Framing languages and literacies: Socially situated views and perspectives* (pp. 136–148). New York: Routledge.

Pahl, K., & Rowsell, J. (2011). Artifactual critical literacy: A new perspective for literacy education. *Berkeley Review of Education*, 2(2), 129–151.

Rinaldi, C. (2006). *In dialogue with Reggio Emilia: Listening, researching and learning*. New York: Routledge.

Rowsell, J. (2013). *Working with multimodality: Rethinking literacy in a digital age*. New York: Routledge.

Share, J. (2009). Young children and critical media literacy. In D. Kellner & R. Hammer (Eds.), *Media/cultural studies: Critical approaches* (pp. 126–151). New York: Peter Lang.

Vasquez, V. (2014). *Negotiating critical literacies with young children 10th anniversary edition*. New York: Routledge-LEA.

Zacher Pandya, J., & Ávila, J. (Eds.). (2014). *Moving critical literacies forward: A new look at praxis across contexts*. New York: Routledge.

Children's Literature Cited

Baguley, E. (2005). *Meggie Moon*. Intercourse, PA: Good Books.

Best, C. (2006). *Sally Jean, the bicycle queen*. New York: Farrar Straus Giroux.

Browne, A. (1990). *Piggybook*. New York: Knopf.

Childerhose, R. J. (1981). The hockey story. Toronto: Nelson Canada.

Clement, R. (1991). *Counting on Frank*. Milwaukee, WI: Gareth Stevens.

Cole, B. (1997). *Princess Smartypants*. New York: Putnam.

Dipuchio, K. (2008). *Grace for president*. New York: Disney Book Group/Hyperion.

Fleischman, P. (2004). *Seed folks*. New York: Harper Teen.

Love, D. A. (2006). *Of numbers and stars: The story of Hypatia*. New York: Holiday House.

Lovell, P., & Catrow, D. (2002). *Stand tall, Molly Lou Melon*. New York: Putnam.

Lyon, G. (1994). *Mama is a miner*. New York: Scholastic.

Mannis, C. D. (2006). *Julia Morgan built a castle*. New York: Viking.

Morrison, T., & Morrison, S. (1999). *The big box*. Burbank, CA: Disney.

Munsch, R. (1988). *The paper bag princess*. Toronto: Annick.

Peet, B. (1991). *The wump world*. New York: Houghton Mifflin.

Perry, S. (1995). *If*. . . Oxford, UK: Oxford University Press Children's Books.

Shange, N. (1997). *White wash*. New York: Walker.

Smith, D. (2002). *If the world were a village: A book about the world's people*. Tonawanda, NY: Kids Can Press.

Smith Milway, K. (2008). *One hen: How one small loan made a big difference*. Tonawanda, NY: Kids Can Press.

Tetro, M. (1994). *The Royal Canadian Mounted Police*. St. Laurent, Quebec: Marc Tetro Canada.

References

Alvermann, D. E., & Hong Xu, S. (2003). Children's everyday literacies: Intersections of popular culture and language arts instruction. *Language Arts*, 81(2), 145–154.

Au, W. (2016). "And Ya Don't Stop": Using hip hop in the language arts classroom. In E. Marshall & Ö. Sensoy (Eds.), *Rethinking popular culture and media* (pp. 277–285). Milwaukee, WI: Rethinking Schools.

Barton, D., & Hamilton, M. (1998). *Local literacies: Reading and writing in one community*. London: Routledge.

Bigelow, W., Christensen, L., Karp, S., Miner, B., & Peterson, B. (1994). *Rethinking our classrooms: Teaching for equity and justice*. Milwaukee, WI: Rethinking Schools.

Buckingham, D., & Sefton-Green, J. (1995). *Cultural studies goes to school: Reading and teaching popular media*. London: Taylor & Francis.

Burke, C. L. (1997). *Using trade books in the classroom*. Graduate seminar, Bloomington, IN: Indiana University.

Christensen, L. (2000). *Reading, writing, and rising up: Teaching about social justice and the power of the written word*. Milwaukee, WI: Rethinking Schools.

Comber, B. (1992). Critical literacy: A selective review and discussion of the recent literature. *South Australian Educational Leader*, 3(1), 1–10.

Comber, B. (1993). Classroom explorations in critical literacy. *Australian Journal of Language and Literacy*, 16(1), 73–83.

Comber, B. (2000). What really counts in early literacy lessons. *Language Arts*, 7(1), 39–49.

Comber, B. (2001a). Critical inquiry or safe literacies: Who's allowed to ask which questions? In S. Boran & B. Comber (Eds.), *Critiquing whole language and classroom inquiry* (pp. 81–102). Urbana, IL: National Council of Teachers of English.

Comber, B. (2001b). Critical literacies and local action: Teacher knowledge and a new research agenda. In B. Comber & A. Simpson (Eds.), *Negotiating critical literacies in classrooms* (pp. 271–282). Mahwah, NJ: Erlbaum.

Comber, B. (2001c). Negotiating critical literacies. *School Talk*, 6(3), 1–3.

Comber, B. (2005). Interview with Barbara Comber. In J. Larson & J. Marsh (Eds.), *Making literacy real: Theories and practices for learning and teaching* (pp. 61–67). Thousand Oaks, CA: Sage.

Comber, B. (2013). Critical literacy in the early years: Emergence and sustenance in an age of accountability. In J. Larson & J. Marsh (Eds.), *The SAGE handbook of early childhood literacy* (pp. 587–601). London: Sage.

Comber, B. (2016). *Literacy, place, and pedagogies of possibility*. New York: Routledge.

Comber, B., & Nixon, H. (2014). Critical literacy across the curriculum: Learning to read, question, and rewrite designs. In J. Zacher Pandya & J. Avila (Eds.), *Moving critical literacies forward: A new look at praxis across contexts* (pp. 83–97). New York: Routledge.

Comber, B., Nixon, H., & Reid, J. (Eds.). (2007). *Literacies in place: Teaching environmental communications*. Newtown, New South Wales, Australia: Primary English Teachers Association.

Comber, B., & Simpson, A. (1995). Reading cereal boxes. In P. Adams & H. Campagna-Wildash (Eds.), *Texts: The heart of the English curriculum* (pp. 1–11). Adelaide, South Australia: Department for Education and Children's Services.

Comber, B., & Simpson, A. (Eds.). (2001). *Negotiating critical literacies in classrooms*. Mahwah, NJ: Erlbaum.

Comber, B., & Thomson, P. (with Wells, M.). (2001). Critical literacy finds a "place": Writing and social action in a low-income Australian grade 2/3 classroom. *The Elementary School Journal*, 101(4), 451–464. doi:10.1086/499681.

Davies, B. (1993). *Shards of glass: Children reading and writing beyond gendered identity*. Sydney: Allen & Unwin.

The Diffusion Group. (2005, May). *Podcasting as an extension of portable digital media: Fact, fiction, and opportunity*. Retrieved September 8, 2006, from www.marketresearch.com/product/display.asp?productid=1150638&g=1

Dyson, A. H. (2003). Popular literacies and the "All" children: Rethinking literacy development for contemporary childhoods. *Language Arts*, 81(2), 100–109.

Edelsky, C. (Ed.). (2000). *Making justice our project: Teachers working toward critical whole language practice*. Urbana, IL: National Council of Teachers of English.

Edmiston, B., & Enciso, P. (2002). Reflections and refractions of meaning: Dialogic approaches to reading withclassroom drama. In J. Flood, D.

Lapp, J.R. Squire & J.M. Jensen (Eds.), *Handbook of research on teaching the English language arts* (pp. 868–880). Mahwah, NJ: Lawrence Erlbaum.

Egawa, K., & Harste, J. C. (2001). Balancing the literary curriculum: A new vision. *School Talk*, 7(1), 1–8.

Enciso, P. (2011). Storytelling in critical literacy pedagogy: Removing the walls between immigrant and non-immigrant youth. In H. Janks & V. Vasquez (Eds.) *Special issue: Critical literacy revisited: Writing as critique for English teaching: Practice and critique*, 10(1), 21–40.

Epstein, D. (1993). *Changing classroom cultures: Anti-racism, politics, and schools*. Stoke-on-Trent, England: Trentham.

Evans, J. (2005). *Literacy Moves On*. Portsmouth, New Hampshire: Heinemann.

Fairclough, N. (1995). *Critical discourse analysis*. London: Longman.

Fiske, J. (1989). *Reading the popular*. London: Routledge.

Freire, P. (1972). *Pedagogy of the oppressed* (M. B. Ramos, Trans.). London: Sheed and Ward.

Freire, P., & Macedo, D. (1987). *Literacy: Reading the word and the world*. South Hadley, MA: Bergin & Garvey.

Galda, L., Rayburn, S., & Stanzi, L. C. (2000). *Looking through the faraway end: Creating a literature-based reading curriculum with second graders*. Newark, DE: International Reading Association.

Gavin, J. (2009). *Global Internet audience surpasses 1 billion visitors*. Retrieved January 3, 2009, from www.comscore.com/Press_Events/Press_Releases/2009/1/Global_Internet_Audience_1_Billion

Gee, J. P. (2003). *What video games have to teach us about learning and literacy*. New York, Palgrave Macmillan.

Gee, J. P. (2004). *Situated language and learning: A critique of traditional schooling*. London: Routledge.

Gee, J. P. (2005). *An introduction to discourse analysis: Theory and method* (2nd ed.). New York: Routledge.

Gilbert, P. (1992). *Gender and literacy: Key issues for the nineties*. Paper prepared for the Victorian Ministry of Education.

Grand'Maison, S. (2008). *Learning from the Beatles* [Presentation]. Podcasters Across Borders Conference, Kingston, Ontario.

Guernsey, L., & Levine, M. H. (2015). *Tap, click, read: Growing readers in a world of screens*. New York: Jossey-Bass.

Haas Dyson, A. (2005). Foreword. In J. Evans (Ed.), *Literacy moves on: Popular culture, new technologies, and critical literacy in the elementary classroom* (pp. ix–xi). Portsmouth, NH: Heinemann.

Halliday, M. A. K. (1978). *Language as social semiotic*. London: Edward Arnold.

Harste, J. C. (1997, July). *Curriculum as audit trail: Underlying premises*. Paper presented at the Whole Language Umbrella Conference, Rochester, New York.

Harste, J. C. (2001, July). *The Halliday plus model*. Presentation given at the 2001 InterLERN Workshop, Mississauga, Ontario, Canada.

Harste, J. C. (2003). What do we mean by literacy now? *Voices from the Middle*, 10(3), 8–12.

Harste, J. C., Leland, C., Lewison, M., Ociepka, A., & Vasquez, V. (2000). Supporting critical conversations in classrooms. In K. M. Pierce (Ed.), *Adventuring with books: A booklist for pre-K–grade 6* (pp. 507–512). Urbana, IL: National Council of Teachers of English.

Heffernan, L., & Lewison, M. (2000). Making real-world issues our business: Critical literacy in a third-grade classroom. *Primary Voices K–6*, 9(2), 15–21.

Heger, D. (2000). *The other meaning of Arbor Day*. Retrieved January 8, 2009, from www.mackinac.org/article.aspx?ID=4126

Janks, H. (1993a). *Language, identity, and power*. Critical Language Awareness Series. Johannesburg: Hodder and Stoughton and Wits University Press.

Janks, H. (1993b). *Language and position*. Critical Language Awareness Series. Johannesburg: Hodder and Stoughton and Wits University Press.

Janks, H. (2000). Domination, access, diversity, and design: A synthesis for critical literacy education. *Educational Review*, 52(2), 175–186. doi:10.1080/713664035.

Janks, H. (2002, November). *Methods, models, and motivations: A synthesis model for critical literacy*. Paper presented at National Council of Teachers of English Annual Convention, Atlanta, GA.

Janks, H. (2010). *Literacy and power*. New York & London: Routledge.

Janks, H. (2014). Critical literacy's ongoing importance for education. *Journal of Adolescent & Adult Literacy*, 57(5), 349–356. Newark, DE: International Reading Association.

Janks, H., & Comber, B. (2005). Critical literacy across continents. In K. Pahl & J. Rowsell (Eds.), *Travel notes from the new literacy studies: Instances of practice* (pp. 95–117). Clevedon, UK: Multilingual Matters.

Janks, H., & Vasquez, V. (Eds.). (2011). *Critical literacy revisited: A special issue of teaching practice and critique*. New Zealand: Waikato University Press.

Johnston, P. (2004). *Choice words: How our language affects children's learning*. Portland, ME: Stenhouse.

Kamler, B. (2001). *Relocating the personal: A critical writing pedagogy*. New York: State University of New York Press.

Kress, G., & Van Leeuwen, T. (2006). *Reading images: The grammar of visual design*. London: Routledge.

Ladson-Billings, G. (1999). Just what is critical race theory and what's it doing in a nice field like education? In L. Parker, D. Deyhle & S. Villenas (Eds.), *Race is . . . race isn't: Critical race theory and qualitative studies in education* (pp. 7–30). New York: Westview.

Ladson-Billings, G. (2003). Foreword. In S. Greene & D. Abt-Perkins (Eds.), *Making race visible: Literacy research for cultural understanding* (pp. vii–xi). New York: Teachers College Press.

Lankshear, C., & Knobel, M. (2007). *A new literacies sampler*. New York: Peter Lang.

Larson, J., & Marsh, J. (2015 [2005]). *Making literacy real: Theories and practices for learning and teaching*. Thousand Oaks, CA: Sage.

Lasseter, J., & Ranft, J. (Directors). (2006). *Cars* [Motion picture]. Emeryville, CA: Disney Pixar Productions.

Lewison, M., Leland, C., Harste, J.C. (2014). *Creating Critical Classrooms: Reading and Writing with an Edge.* New York: Routledge.

Luke, A. (1998). Getting over method: Literacy teaching as work in new times. *Language Arts*, 75(4), 3–13.

Luke, A. (2007). *The new literacies*. Webcasts and Podcasts for Educators, Toronto, ON: Curriculum Services Canada. Retrieved January 20, 2009, from www.curriculum.org/secretariat/may31.shtml

Luke, A. (2013). Regrounding critical literacy: Representation, facts and reality. In M. Hawkins (Ed.), *Framing languages and literacies: Socially situated views and perspectives* (pp. 136–148). New York: Routledge.

Luke, A. (2014). Defining critical literacy. In J. Zacher Pandya & J. Avila (Eds.), *Moving critical literacies forward: A new look at praxis across contexts* (pp. 19–31). New York & London: Routledge/Taylor & Francis.

Luke, A., & Freebody, P. (1997). Shaping the social practices of reading. In S. Muspratt, A. Luke & P. Freebody (Eds.), *Constructing critical literacies: Teaching and learning textual practice* (pp. 185–226). Cresskill, NJ: Hampton.

Luke, A., & Freebody, P. (1999a). A map of possible practices: Further notes on the four resources model. *Practically Primary*, 4(2), 5–8.

Luke, A., & Freebody, P. (1999b). Further notes on the four resources model. *Reading online*. Retrieved July 15, 2000, from www.readingonline.org/research/lukefreebody.html

Luke, A., O'Brien, J., & Comber, B. (1994). Making community texts objects of study. *Australian Journal of Language and Literacy*, 17(2), 139–149.

Manning, A. (1993). Curriculum as conversation. In A. Manning (Ed.), *Foundations of literacy* (pp. 48–60). Halifax, Nova Scotia: Mount Saint Vincent University.

Marsh, J. (Ed.). (2005). *Popular culture, new media and digital literacy in early childhood*. New York: Routledge Falmer.

Meacham, S. J. (2003, March). *Literacy and street credibility: Plantations, prisons, and African American literacy from Frederick Douglass to fifty cent*. Presentation at the Economic and Social Research Council Seminar Series Conference, Sheffield, United Kingdom.

Medina, C. L. (2006). Identity and imagination of immigrant children: Creating common place locations in literary interpretation. In J. Jasinski Schneider, T.P. Crumpler & T. Rogers (Eds.), *Process drama and multiple literacies: Addressing social, cultural, and ethical issues* (pp. 53–70). Portsmouth, NH: Heinemann.

Medina, C. L., & Wohlwend, K. E. (2014). *Literacy, play and globalization: Converging imaginaries in children's critical and cultural performances*. New York: Routledge.

Mitchell, R. (2016). School days: Hail, hail, rock 'n' roll! In E. Marshall & Ö. Sensoy (Eds.), *Rethinking popular culture and media* (pp. 167–174). Milwaukee, WI: Rethinking Schools.

Moll, L. C. (1992). Funds of knowledge for teaching: Using a qualitative approach to connect homes and classrooms. *Theory into Practice*, 31(1), 132–141.

Morgan, W. (1997). *Critical literacy in the classroom: The art of the possible.* New York: Routledge.

Morrell, E. (2008). *Critical literacy and urban youth: Pedagogies of access, dissent, and liberation*. New York: Routledge.

Morrell, E., & Duncan-Andrade, J. (2002). Promoting academic literacy with urban youth through engaging hip-hop culture. *English Journal*, 91(6), 88–92.

The New London Group. (1996). A pedagogy of multiliteracies: Designing social futures. *Harvard Education Review*, 66(1), 60–92.

Nixon, H. (2003). New research literacies for contemporary research into literacy and new media? *Reading Research Quarterly*, 38(4), 407–413.

Nixon, H., & Comber, B. (2005). Behind the scenes: Making movies in early years classrooms. In J. Marsh (Ed.), *Popular culture, media and digital literacies in early childhood* (pp. 219–236). New York: Routledge.

Nixon, A. S., & Gutiérrez, K. (2008). Digital literacies for young English learners: Productive pathways toward equity and robust learning. In C. Genishi & A. L. Goodwin (Eds.), *Diversities in early childhood education: Rethinking and doing* (pp. 121–136). New York: Routledge.

O'Brien, J. (1998). Experts in Smurfland. In M. Knobel & A. Healy (Eds.), *Critical literacy in the primary classroom* (pp. 13–25). Newtown, New South Wales, Australia: Primary English Teaching Association.

O'Brien, J. (2001). Children reading critically: A local history. In B. Comber & A. Simpson (Eds.), *Negotiating critical literacies in classrooms* (pp. 37–54). Mahwah, NJ: Erlbaum. Oxford University Press. (2005).

O'Neill, C., & Lambert, A. (1983). *Drama Structures: A Practical Handbook for Teachers*. Portsmouth, NH: Heinemann.

Pahl, K., & Rowsell, J. (2011). Artifactual critical literacy: A new perspective for literacy education. *Berkeley Review of Education*, 2(2), 129–151.

Rinaldi, C. (2006). *In dialogue with Reggio Emilia: Listening, researching and learning*. New York: Routledge.

Rowe, D. W. (2005). Suggestions for further reading on literacy learning and the young child. *Language Arts*, 82(4), 324.

Rowsell, J. (2013). *Working with multimodality: Rethinking literacy in a digital age*. New York: Routledge.

Scheibe, C. L., & Rogow, F. (2011). *The teacher's guide to media literacy: Critical thinking in a multimedia world*. New York: Corwin.

Schmidt, K. (1998, August). *Math Investigations*. Presentation given at the 1998 InterLERN Workshop, Mississauga, Ontario, Canada.

Share, J. (2009). Young children and critical media literacy. In D. Kellner & R. Hammer (Eds.), *Media/cultural studies: Critical approaches* (pp. 126–151). New York: Peter Lang.

Share, J. (2010). Voices from the trenches: Elementary school teachers speak about implementing media literacy. In K. Tyner (Ed.), *Media literacy: New agendas in communication* (pp. 53–75). New York: Routledge.

Share, J. (2015). *Media literacy is elementary: Teaching youth to critically read and create media* (2nd ed., Rethinking Childhood). New York: Peter Lang.

Shor, I., & Freire, P. (1987). *A pedagogy for liberation: Dialogues on transforming education*. South Hadley, MA: Bergin & Garvey.

Short, K. G., Harste, J. C., & Burke, C. L. (1996). *Creating classrooms for authors and inquirers*. Portsmouth, NH: Heinemann.

Tate, S. (2011). Equity and access through literacy development and instruction: The use of critical text to transform student writing and identity within a research seminar. In H. Janks & V. Vasquez (Eds.), *Special issue: Critical literacy revisited: Writing as critique for English teaching: Practice and critique*, 10(1), 199–208.

Vasquez, V. (1994). A step in the dance of critical literacy. *UKRAReading*, 28(1), 39–43. Oxford, UK: Blackwell.

Vasquez, V. (1998). Building equitable communities: Taking social action in a kindergarten classroom. *Talking Points*, 9(2), 3–6.

Vasquez, V. (2000a). Language stories and critical literacy lessons. *Talking Points*, 11(2), 5–8. Urbana, IL: National Council of Teachers of English.

Vasquez, V. (2000b). Our way: Using the everyday to create a critical literacy curriculum. *Primary Voices*, 9(2), 8–13. Urbana, IL: National Council of Teachers of English.

Vasquez, V. (2000c). Building community through social action. *School Talk*, 5(4), 2–3.

Vasquez, V. (2001a). Classroom inquiry into the incidental unfolding of social justice issues: Seeking out possibilities in the lives of learners. In B. Comber & S. Cakmac (Eds.), *Critiquing whole language and classroom inquiry* (pp. 200–215). Urbana, IL: National Council of Teachers of English.

Vasquez, V. (2001b). Negotiating critical literacies in elementary classrooms. In B. Comber & S. Cakmac (Eds.), *Critical literacy at elementary sites* (pp. 55–66). Mahwah, NJ: Lawrence Erlbaum.

Vasquez, V. (2001c). Creating a critical literacy curriculum with young children. *Phi Delta Kappa International Research Bulletin*, 29(1), 1–4.

Vasquez, V. (2003a). *Using the everyday: Constructing critical literacies with young children*. Mahwah, NJ: Erlbaum.

Vasquez, V. (2003b). *Negotiating critical literacies with young children*. Mahwah, NJ: Lawrence Erlbaum.

Vasquez, V. (2003c). What Pokemon can teach us about learning and literacy. *Language Arts*, 81(2), 118–125.

Vasquez, V. (2004). *Negotiating critical literacies with young children*. New York: Routledge.

Vasquez, V. (2005a). Creating spaces for critical literacy with young children: Using everyday issues and everyday text. In J. Evans (Ed.), *Literacy moves on* (pp. 78–97). David Fulton (UK) and Heinemann (USA).

Vasquez, V. (2005b). Resistance, power-tricky, and colorless energy: What engagement with everyday popular culture texts can teach us about learning, and literacy. In J. Marsh (Ed.), *Popular culture, new media and digital literacy in early childhood* (pp. 201–218). New York: Routledge Falmer.

Vasquez, V. (2010). iPods, puppy dogs, and podcasts: Imagining literacy instruction for the 21st century. *School Talk*, 15(2), 1–2.

Vasquez, V. (2014a). Re-designing critical literacies. In J. Zacher Pandya & J. Ávila (Eds.), *Moving critical literacies forward: A new look at praxis across contexts* (pp. 174–186). New York: Routledge.

Vasquez, V. (2014b). *Negotiating critical literacies with young children 10th anniversary edition*. New York: Routledge-LEA.

Vasquez, V. (2017). *Critical literacy across the curriculum in K–6 settings*. New York: Routledge.

Vasquez, V., Egawa, K., Harste, J. C., & Thompson, R. (Eds.). (2004). *Literacy as social practice: Primary voices K–6*. Urbana, IL: National Council of Teachers of English.

Vasquez, V., & Felderman, C. (2013). *Technology and critical literacy in early childhood*. New York: Routledge.

Vasquez, V., Tate, S. L., & Harste, J. C. (2013). *Negotiating critical literacies with teachers*. New York: Routledge.

Vicars, M. (2013). Queerer than queer. In J. N. Lester & R. Gabriel (Eds.), *Performances of research critical issues in K–12 education*. New York: Peter Lang.

Virginia Department of Education. (n.d.). *Standards of learning currently in effect for Virginia public schools*. Retrieved November 1, 2008, from www.doe.virginia.gov/VDOE/Superintendent/Sols/home.shtml

Watson, R. (2016). The murder of Sean Bell from pain to poetry. In E. Marshall & Ö. Sensoy (Eds.), *Rethinking popular culture and media* (pp. 270–276). Milwaukee, WI: Rethinking Schools.

Watson, D., Burke, C. L., & Harste, J. C. (1989). *Whole language: Inquiring voices*. New York: Scholastic.

Whitin, P., & Whitin, D. J. (2000). *Math is language too: Talking and writing in the mathematics classroom*. Urbana, IL: National Council of Teachers of English; Reston, VA: National Council of Teachers of Mathematics.

Whitin, D. J., & Whitin, P. (2004). *New visions for linking literature and mathematics*. Urbana, IL: National Council of Teachers of English; Reston, VA: National Council of Teachers of Mathematics.

Whitin, D. J., & Whitin, P. (2005). *What if we changed the book? Problem-posing with sixteen cows*. Retrieved June 16, 2009, from www.readwritethink.org/lessons/lesson_view.asp?id=815

Wohlwend, K. E. (2013). *Literacy playshop: New literacies, popular media, and play in the early childhood classroom*. New York: Teachers College Press.

Index

Note. Page numbers followed by *f* or *t* indicate figures or tables, respectively